INVOLVEMENT IN PSYCHOLOGY TODAY   SECOND EDITION

CONTRIBUTING CONSULTANT

Robert Merrill Springer, who earned his
B.A. and M.A. from California State College in Los Angeles, is in his fourth year
of graduate studies at the University of
California in San Diego. Mr. Springer returned to academic life after spending
several years as a human factors specialist
at North American Aviation. He is concentrating his studies on perception and
perceptual development.

INVOLVEMENT IN
Psychology Today
SECOND EDITION

 CRM BOOKS
DEL MAR, CALIFORNIA

To the Student

This is an antiwork book. It was built to be your weapon against drudgery.

You learn best by doing and by making mistakes. *Involvement in Psychology Today,* Second Edition, provides you with things to do and with opportunities to make mistakes. We have outlined the projects, but you will create the details and discover the answers. This is not a workbook that spoonfeeds knowledge; this is an action book for individuals who can take an idea and make it work by getting involved.

In some cases, the intent is to invite you to examine controversial ideas critically and to discover the personal and social implications of the subject matter. But perhaps of greatest importance, this book is designed to help the student find out about himself.

Contents

Methodology

Any student alone will have difficulty obtaining large groups of people for experiments. Therefore, when large amounts of data are most helpful, pool your results with the data of your classmates. Each time the class pools its data, one person can be responsible for all data. Each student can then collect only a small amount of data and turn it over to the designated person, who can mimeograph the results.

Determining Correlations

A method of discovering how one event relates to another is to determine the correlation between the events. Correlations can be as low as zero or as high as −1.0 or +1.0. The number tells us the strength of the relationship, and the sign (plus or minus) indicates the direction (positive or negative) of the correlation. Height and weight correlate about +.80, which means that tall people tend to be heavier than short people. The plus sign tells us that a high score on event A (height) will be accompanied by a high score on event B (weight). Amount of training in typing skills probably correlates about −.70 with typing errors. The minus sign indicates that a high score on event A (training) means a low score on event B (errors). Height and typing errors probably correlate about .00 which means that a high score on event A (height) doesn't tell us anything about event B (errors).

Using data on actual heights and weights, we can make a pictorial representation of the correlation, called a scatterplot. For example, if we measured the heights and weights of eight males and found the following information, we could then plot the data as shown in Figure 0.1.

Subject	Height (inches)	Weight (lbs.)
1	73	212
2	63	150
3	69	165
4	76	214
5	70	180
6	71	190
7	72	210
8	70½	185

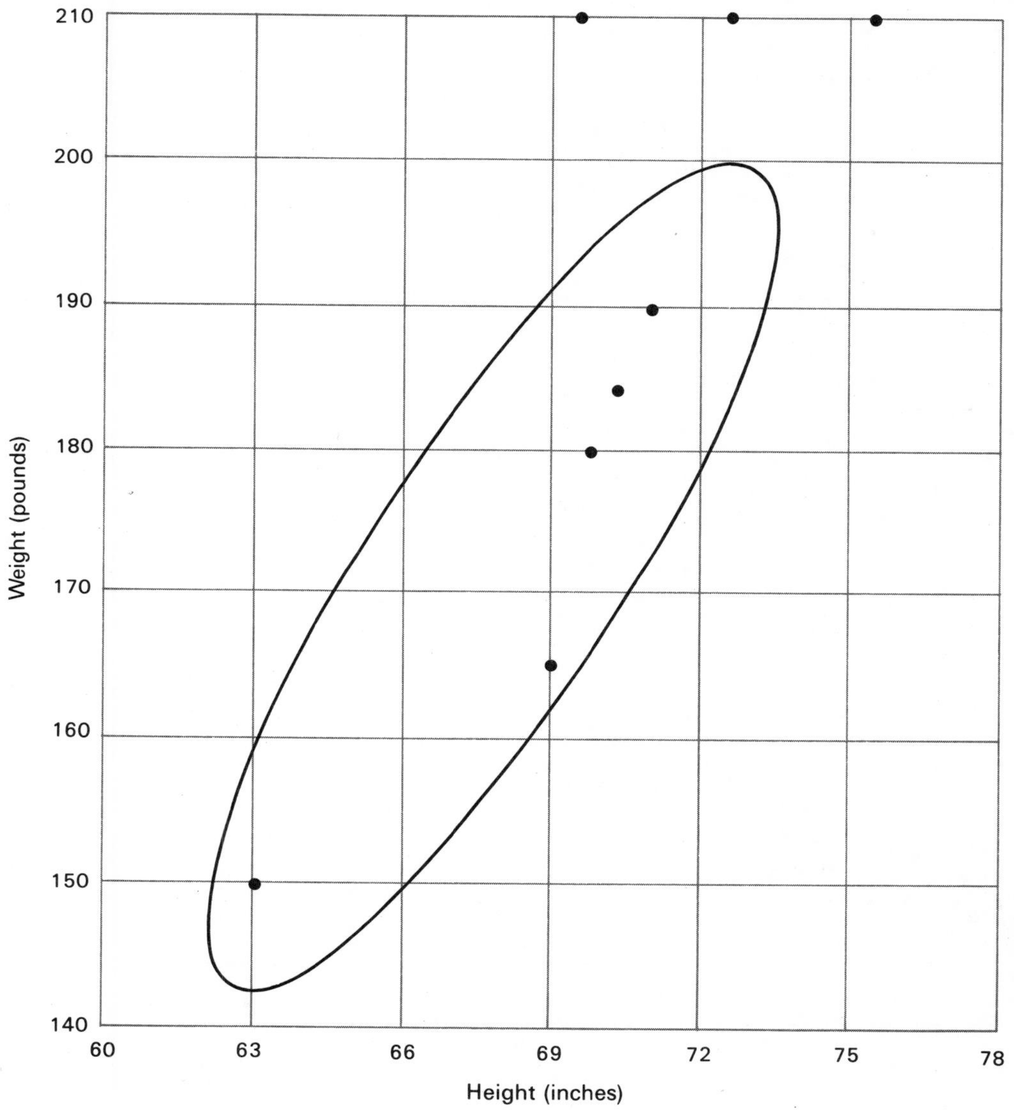

Figure 0.1. This scatter-plot shows the correlation between the height and weight data listed. This representation allows one to see at a glance that weight and height are positively correlated, the correlation being about +.80.

The ellipse drawn through the points gives a pictorial estimation of the correlation strength, as well as giving the sign (+ or −) of the correlation. The correlation in Figure 0.1 is about +.80. Several other scatterplots with estimated correlations are shown in Figure 0.2.

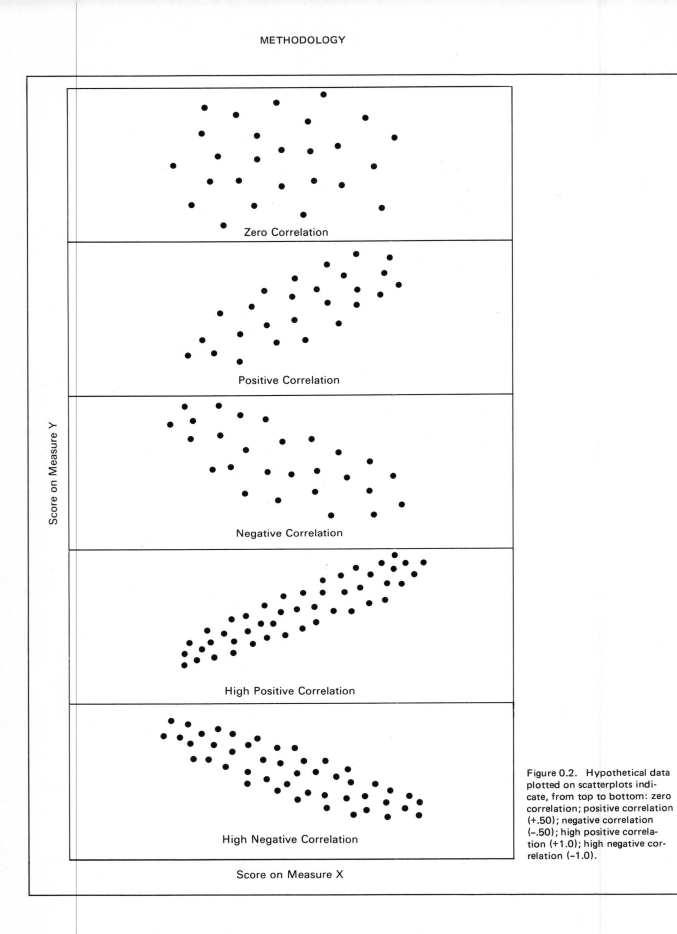

Figure 0.2. Hypothetical data plotted on scatterplots indicate, from top to bottom: zero correlation; positive correlation (+.50); negative correlation (−.50); high positive correlation (+1.0); high negative correlation (−1.0).

You can calculate a correlation very simply with the Spearman rho formula:

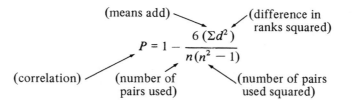

$$P = 1 - \frac{6\,(\Sigma d^2)}{n\,(n^2 - 1)}$$

(means add) — (difference in ranks squared)

(correlation) — (number of pairs used) — (number of pairs used squared)

To determine the correlation of the height-weight data shown at the bottom of page x, follow these simple steps:

(1) Rank order the data:

Height (inches)		Rank	Weight		Rank
73		2	212		2
63	(shortest)	8	150	(lightest)	8
69		7	165		7
76	(tallest)	1	214	(heaviest)	1
70		6	180		6
71		4	210		3
72		3	185		5
70½		5	190		4

(2) Obtain, square, and add the differences in the ranks:

Height rank	Weight rank	d (ht. rank minus wt. rank)	d^2
2	2	0	0
8	8	0	0
7	7	0	0
1	1	0	0
6	6	0	0
4	3	1	1
3	5	-2	4
5	4	1	1
			6

(3) Determine the values for n and n^2

$$n = \text{ 8 pairs}$$
$$n^2 = 64$$
$$n^2 - 1 = 63$$

(4) Insert your data into the formula and work the problem.

$$P = 1 - \frac{6\,(\Sigma d^2)}{n(n^2 - 1)}$$

$$P = 1 - \frac{6\,(6)}{8\,(63)} = 1 - \frac{36}{504} = (\text{approx.}) + .93$$

You will be asked to make use of this method and the Spearman rho formula later in this book, so it might be a good idea to read through this section once more to make sure you understand the fairly simple process of determining correlations.

INVOLVEMENT IN PSYCHOLOGY TODAY   SECOND EDITION

To understand psychology we must first understand science, for the psychologist is a scientist.

The goal of science is the understanding of our universe. The psychologist is a scientist who has dedicated himself to understanding a small portion of that universe—man.

The scientist cannot understand his world without collecting information. He tries to do so in a manner that is *reliable*—that is, capable of replication. When he manipulates some *independent variable* (the factor he changes), some *dependent variable* (the change made by the independent variable) changes in value. Because he is aware that his perceptions (conscious awareness) of the outcome of the experiment may differ from that of another person, he tries to collect his information as *objectively* as possible, so others would get the same information from the observation.

There are two ways in which the scientist increases his objectivity so that others can repeat his experiment and arrive at the same information: (a) He defines his independent and dependent variables *operationally*—that is, in terms of the concrete operations he used to change or measure the variable. For example, the operational definition of "hunger" might be numbers of hours of deprivation; the dependent variable in an experiment using hunger as a "drive" might be how hard an animal pulls on a harness to get food. (b) The scientist uses *instruments* to measure his dependent variable, so that other observers can obtain data with little interobserver variation. Thus, using a digital thermometer will probably elicit more agreement among observers than will estimating an object's temperature by touch.

The scientist cannot study all the variables in the universe simultaneously; therefore, he limits the number of independent variables he manipulates at any one time and *controls* (freezes or negates) the effects of all other variables. To the extent that a scientist controls for *extraneous* variables (not important in the experiment), he will have to limit the generalities he draws from his findings. Another factor that limits the generality of an experiment is the level of reduction. By limiting the number of variables he investigates, the scientist usually chooses to study effects somewhere along the continuum from atomistic (microscopic facets of the object under study) to holistic (global aspects, such as a society or a galaxy). A trade-off exists, therefore, between the complexity of the variables studied and the generality of the scientist's conclusions: The more controlled an experiment, the less general; or, the less controlled, the more complicated. Moreover, the scientist usually must limit his generalizations to the level of reduction he has chosen; for the same reason, a mechanic probably does not base his diagnosis of your car's condition on knowledge of motion in the metal molecules.

Much of the scientist's data is gathered in experiments, conducted in controlled settings. However, many scientists—and particularly psychologists—obtain data in natural settings by observing natural phenomena. The scientist has much less control over variables in a natural environment, but he can, nevertheless, often obtain valuable information.

The most important step in the scientific process occurs after the scientist has gathered his data; he must then formulate a theory or principle to explain why the manipulation of the independent variable led to changes in the dependent variable, or why his input produced a certain output. This mystical process, which is poorly understood and often called creativity, is formally called *induction*. The scientist looks at his results and thinks about what he did and somehow "induces," or arrives

1
Introduction: Philosophy of the Science of Psychology

at, the conclusion that a particular principle is operating. The scientist tests his principle by formulating hypotheses and testing them. Thus, if he wants to test a theory that light slows down in dense substances, he might formulate the hypothesis that a wedge of glass will bend light rays; to the extent that the rays bend, his theory is supported. If this hypothesis is incorrect, his theory is probably wrong. When a theory has been verified many times, it is often called a law.

Scientists often rely upon concepts in their theories that describe the linkage of independent to dependent variables; these concepts are called *intervening variables*. For example, scientists talk about magnetism although they cannot tell you what it is, and they speak of atomic particles without ever having seen a single atom. Intervening variables are difficult to define operationally and are usually defined in terms of independent and dependent variables. They are useful to the extent that many independent variables lead to the same intervening variable or a single intervening variable leads to many dependent variables. As an example, consider the general principle that when electricity (an independent variable) flows through a coil wrapped around an iron bar, the iron bar will pick up (dependent variable) a thumb tack. How much simpler to posit an intervening variable—magnetism—to account not only for the coil lifting a thumb tack but for its capacity to move other iron-bearing metals as well. Thus, the coil will also pick up a paper clip and, if powerful enough, a car. Moreover, a bar magnet will also pick up the tack. Thus, all the independent variables are connected to all the dependent variables by one convenient intervening variable—magnetism. Intervening variables are useful to the extent they help generalize from a large amount of data to a large number of hypotheses or predictions; that is, to the extent they make a theory more general.

Science, then, is the business of trying to derive principles, each of which explains as much of the phenomena of the universe as possible.

THE PSYCHOLOGIST AS A SCIENTIST

Psychologists spend a great deal of time trying to convince themselves and others that they are scientists. This preoccupation results from the psychologist's decision to study man's behavior, which is so complicated that it often eludes efforts to catalogue and measure it using known scientific methods.

As a scientist, the psychologist seeks to derive principles of human behavior. The psychologist's first task must be, therefore, the scientist's first task—to gather objective, reliable data about his subject of interest. It is here that the psychologist encounters many of the complexities he must deal with. The inputs the average human processes *and* the behaviors (including internal mental processes) he generates are remarkably numerous and complicated. Consequently, the psychologist often has trouble limiting his variables to a few (that is, setting up controls) and operationally defining his independent and dependent variables. Moreover, many of the dependent variables he measures are either unreliable, difficult to reconstruct with the same value, or—as with consciousness—difficult to measure with instruments. However, like any scientist, the psychologist can often exercise the controls necessary to reduce the number of variables to a manageable few. This challenge absorbs the experimental psychologist. With some persistence, he can operationally define his independent and dependent variables. "Fear," for example, can be defined by the conditions that give rise to it, such as "seeing an unexpected object." (Of course, "unexpected" would have to be pinned down a bit.)

One of the psychologist's greatest challenges is to measure his dependent variable in such a way that another psychologist would obtain the same information. He must often settle for highly variable data. Dealing with such data is the job of the statistician. The dependent variable he is interested in may be impossible to assess by other than somewhat indirect measures; for example, "emotion" is often measured by skin resistance, verbal report ("I'm scared"), or some other indirect manifestation.

PSYCHOLOGICAL THEORIZING

The psychologist either collects his data in a naturalistic setting or conducts an experiment in which controls exist. He manipulates independent variables and measures dependent variables. After he has gathered his data, the psychologist faces the task of *inducing* general principles (theories) to explain the behavior of his subjects. The psychologist usually also makes use of intervening variables in his theories. Thus, after collecting a large amount of data in fairly naturalistic settings, Freud posited the intervening variables of id, ego, and superego. These three variables, not directly observable, provide a bridge from observable inputs (independent variables) to observable outputs (dependent variables or indirect indications of dependent variables). The fact that no one has ever seen an ego does not diminish its importance. It is a valuable construct to the extent it helps tie input to output. Thus, for example, if a person is shamed in the presence of a loved one (an independent variable), the psychologist can predict some dependent variable; for example, the shamed person may blush or become angry.

Intervening variables are valuable to the extent they help the psychologist formulate theories that lead to demonstrable hypotheses. In general, a theory is confirmed to the extent it leads to confirmable hypotheses. One of the major obstacles the psychologist confronts is in making testable hypotheses from his theories. To the extent a theory is untestable, it is not valuable to the scientist, although that theory may be a true model of the way things operate. Freud's theories are so complicated, and in some cases diffuse, that they have been criticized for being incapable of generating specific predictions or for leading to conflicting predictions. Much of Freud's work, however, has led to correct predictions. A theory in psychology may not be demonstrable (or even totally correct) and still be valuable, simply because it has led to accurate predictions more frequently than any other theory. But, like any scientist, the psychologist must be cautious about generalizing beyond his experiment or to a different level of reduction.

The psychologist, then, is a scientist in that he derives his principles through the scientific method. Of course, not all psychologists are in the business of formulating new laws of behavior; that is the job of researchers. Some psychologists, such as counselors, are totally applied in their use of psychology. In some ways, they have the same relationship to research psychologists as mechanical engineers have to physicists.

DESIGNING AN EXPERIMENT

You wish to determine whether or not a young child can be taught to hate pink rabbits. Would you use naturalistic observation or an experiment?

What would your independent and dependent variables be? How would your terms be defined and dependent on the variable measured? What controls would you use?

Could you derive a principle (theory) from this experiment, if it turned out to be valid? What intervening variables would you use in your principle? How far could you generalize your findings?

DETERMINING WHAT IS TESTABLE

Several theories are presented below. Can you tell which might be untestable? For which would the terms be difficult to operationally define?

(1) A person will remember an unfinished task.
(2) Love reduces hate.
(3) You can raise blood pressure by making a subject anxious.
(4) Motivation increases learning.
(5) Making a rat hungry will cause him to require less training on a maze task.

ETHICS AND THE SCIENTIFIC METHOD

Where do social values and needs fit into the scientific method? Suppose a scientist has information that could be harmful to society. Should he feel any obligation to withhold his findings?

SUGGESTED READINGS

Combs, A. W., and Snygg, D. *Individual Behavior: a Perceptual Approach to Behavior*. New York, Harper & Row, 1959. Contains good philosophical discussion of *levels of analysis* by two of America's pioneer phenomenologists.

Chomsky, N. *Language and Mind*. New York, Harcourt Brace Jovanovich, 1968. Much of this book is too complicated for nonlinguists, but it contains an excellent section on evidence for holistic learning.

Hampden-Turner, C. *Radical Man: the Process of Psychosocial Development*. Garden City, N. Y., Anchor Books, 1971. Presents a convincing case in the opening chapter that the ramifications of behaviorism in social life are conservative and antidevelopmental.

Homans, G. C. *The Nature of Social Science*. New York, Harbinger, 1967. A small gem of clarity and conviction by a pro-behaviorist sociologist.

Kaplan, A. *The Conduct of Inquiry: Methodology for Behavioral Science*. San Francisco, Chandler Publishing, 1964. Probably the best-written, most coherent and comprehensive review in the English language of methodological and philosophical issues by one of America's greatest teachers. He demonstrates the close connection between behaviorism and the most fruitful axioms of the physical sciences.

Koestler, A. *The Act of Creation*. New York, Macmillan, 1966. A *tour de force* on human and even animal creativity. Very critical of behaviorism.

Kuhn, T. S. *The Structure of Scientific Revolutions*. Chicago, University of Chicago Press, 1970. The historian of science who argues that science proceeds by periodic conceptual revolutions in its philosophy of science. The implication is that we are due for one!

Matson, F. W. *The Broken Image: Man, Science and Society*. Garden City, N.Y., Anchor Books, 1966. Shows that the physical sciences are increasingly bringing humans back into their perspectives. Argues that any science must rest upon the wholeness, dignity, and worth of its subject matter. Excellent for historical background and comparative sciences.

Natanson, M. (Ed.). *Philosophy of the Social Sciences: A Reader*. New York, Random House, 1963. A most skillfully excerpted book that presents the conflicting views of Jonas, Nagel, Winch, Hempel, Shutz, Ayer, and Merleau-Ponty.

UNIT I
Learning

2 Instinctive Behavior

How can we tell where instinct leaves off and intelligent behavior begins? A child learns to speak early with a minimum of training, yet he takes much longer to learn to read, although he is surrounded by words. Moreover, it seems much more difficult for adults to learn foreign languages than for children, as if a critical period akin to that in imprinting exists for spoken language. Do you think talking and other intelligent acts have instinctive components? Consider in your answer:

fixed action   neural stimulation
flexibility   vacuum behavior
displacement   sign stimuli releasers

AGGRESSION

Konrad Lorenz argues that man is instinctively aggressive. How is Lorenz contradicted by the influence of learning in predisposing individuals to aggression and by cross-cultural differences in the types and degrees of aggression tolerated?

How would you design an experiment to test Lorenz's contentions?

THE TERRITORIAL IMPERATIVE

In *The Territorial Imperative*, Robert Ardrey notes that most animals establish territorial boundaries that they defend against intruders. What determines these boundaries and what purposes do they serve? Can you think of various displacement activities that might take place when an intruder enters foreign territory?

Watch the behavior of dogs in a local neighborhood. Determine what each dog considers to be the boundary of his territory. Observe other animals to see if each one stakes out a territory that he defends against others of his own kind. Does he defend this territory against other species?

Explore the existence of the territorial imperative in human beings:

Ask a married man what he would do if he was out with his wife and a strange man tried to become friendly with her.

Walk up to a secretary you do not know, open up one of her desk drawers, and take a piece of paper.

Ask a physician how he reacts when a patient makes a self-diagnosis and demands a specific medicine. (Watch what happens any time an "amateur" intrudes into an "expert's" field.)

Find a man sitting in his parked car and sit down on the fender of the car.

Walk up to a woman and drop a paper clip into her purse.

Walk through a dormitory until you see a student you do not know. Go into his room, sit down on his bed, and start reading a book.

SPECIES-SPECIFIC BEHAVIOR

The psychologist must recognize when behavior is species-specific. For example, rats depend more on their olfactory equipment than do humans and also have more difficulty avoiding painful stimuli. In such cases, should we avoid generalizing from the results of experiments with animals to speculations about human behavior?

Another problem with cross-species generalizations is that the individual animals used for experimental purposes live in very restricted environments, probably never having been outside a laboratory setting. It is not surprising that lab animals will endure pain to obtain food; they have been starved beforehand. In addition, research has shown that sensory deprivation destroys mental behavior in animals. Where should psychologists draw the line in generalizing from animal to human behavior?

SUGGESTED READINGS

Darwin, C. *Expression of the Emotions in Man and Animals.* Chicago, University of Chicago Press, 1965. With this book, originally published in 1872, Darwin developed the assumption that an animal's behavior is characteristic of its species, in the same way that its bodily characteristics are.

Eibl-Eibesfeldt, I. *Ethology. The Biology of Behavior.* New York, Holt, Rinehart & Winston, 1970. A useful, up-to-date introductory survey on the field of ethology, written by a student and colleague of Konrad Lorenz.

Frisch, K. von. *The Dance Language and Orientation of Bees.* Cambridge, Mass., Belknap Press of Harvard University Press, 1967. Von Frisch's most recent and most extensive treatment of his lifetime of work with honeybees.

Lorenz, K. *Evolution and Modification of Behavior.* Chicago, University of Chicago Press, 1965. In this short book, Lorenz analyzes the meaning of the term "innate" as applied to behavior and discusses controversies over the heredity of behavior.

Lorenz, K. *King Solomon's Ring.* New York, Thomas Y. Crowell, 1952. A light, easy-to-read book of essays about Lorenz's many interesting experiences with animals.

Lorenz, K. *Studies in Animal and Human Behavior.* Vol. I. Cambridge, Mass., Harvard University Press, 1970. Lorenz's most important papers are being brought together in English translation in several volumes.

Marler, P. R., and Hamilton, W. J. *Mechanisms of Animal Behavior.* New York, Wiley, 1966. A thorough, well-written summary and integration of major areas of research on animal behavior.

Roe, A., and Simpson, G. (Eds.). *Behavior and Evolution.* New Haven, Conn., Yale University Press, 1958. A collection of papers by important researchers in the field of behavior and evolution.

Thorpe, W. H. *Learning and Instinct in Animals.* 2nd ed. Cambridge, Mass., Harvard Univeristy Press, 1963. An important treatment of ethological research on the nature of learning in different species of animals.

Tinbergen, N. *The Study of Instinct.* New York, Oxford University Press, 1969. A stimulating discussion of instinctive behavior by one of the most important modern ethologists.

3
Conditioning and Learning

Behaviorists circumscribe the data of psychology to observable phenomena. If psychologists were to study only observable behavior, how would the following topics be investigated?

consciousness and thinking
psychopathology and neurosis
perception
emotions and motivation

CLASSICAL CONDITIONING: THE EYE BLINK

Two primary types of conditioning have been distinguished: operant and classical. Operant is easily observed—reading this manual for knowledge or for fear of a bad grade are forms of operant conditioning; avoiding a bad grade or acquiring knowledge are reinforcements. Classical conditioning can be demonstrated as follows:

Puff gently through a straw at your subject's eye, causing the subject to blink, as shown in Figure 3.1. About one second before each puff, make a loud sound, by banging on a pot or ringing a buzzer, for example. After twenty to thirty such pairings, stop puffing (the unconditioned stimulus) but continue making the sound (the conditioned stimulus). If conditioning has occurred, the sound alone will elicit an eye blink (conditioned response). Keep generating the sound; at a certain point the sound should no longer elicit the eye blink. Eliminating the unconditioned stimulus has extinguished the conditioned response.

HABITUATION

Puff a pulse of air softly through a straw at a partner's eye. The subject should blink. Keep puffing. If the eye blink eventually ceases, habituation has occurred. Let the subject rest. Resume the eyeblink trials. The eyeblink response will probably have returned; if so, the behavior has spontaneously recovered.

What role might classical conditioning play in developing the following traits?

emotions	feelings of national pride
prejudices	religious beliefs

OPERANT CONDITIONING—HOW A RAT FEELS

Construct the viewing apparatus as described on page 14. Ask someone to learn the maze in Figure 3.2. by looking through your viewer; your subject should be able to see only an alley and part of a wall at one time. Have the subject call out the cul-de-sacs as he comes to them until he learns the maze. Run him through it until he can do the maze without errors, arriving at the proper cul-de-sac four out of four times. Keep track of the time taken for each trial, the number of errors, and where the errors occurred.

To find out if a relationship exists between time taken to learn the maze and errors, correlate time with errors. A high correlation means a strong relationship.

In what order were errors eliminated, or what was the serial position effect?

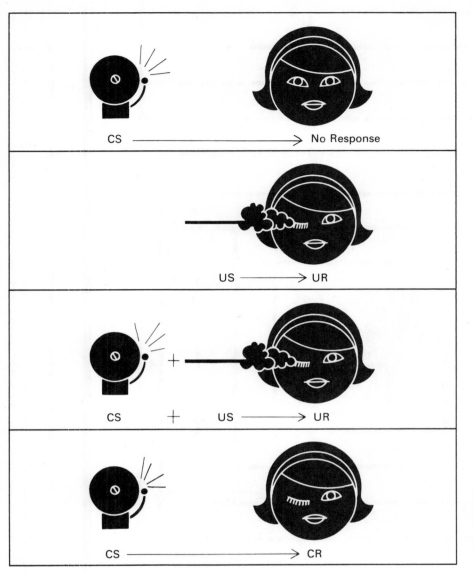

CS ——————————→ No Response

US ——————→ UR

CS   +   US ——————→ UR

CS ——————————→ CR

Figure 3.1. To elicit the eye blink for the classical conditioning procedure, puff *gently* through a drinking straw, as shown. It is crucial that the sound (conditioned stimulus) *precede* the puffing (unconditioned stimulus). If it follows the puffing, conditioning will not occur.

Did your subject reach a perfect run and then make an error on the next run? If so, can you now see the wisdom of running four out of four as the criterion of learning?

CONDITIONING IN EVERYDAY LIFE

Does pure operant conditioning ever occur without classical conditioning? (Hint: When a rat runs a maze for food, his mouth waters near the goal.)

Cite examples in everyday life when you are under stimulus control. For example, superstitious behavior at the dice table is a form of stimulus control. What are some examples of conditioned reinforcers in your daily life? When is shaping used to mold your behavior?

START HERE

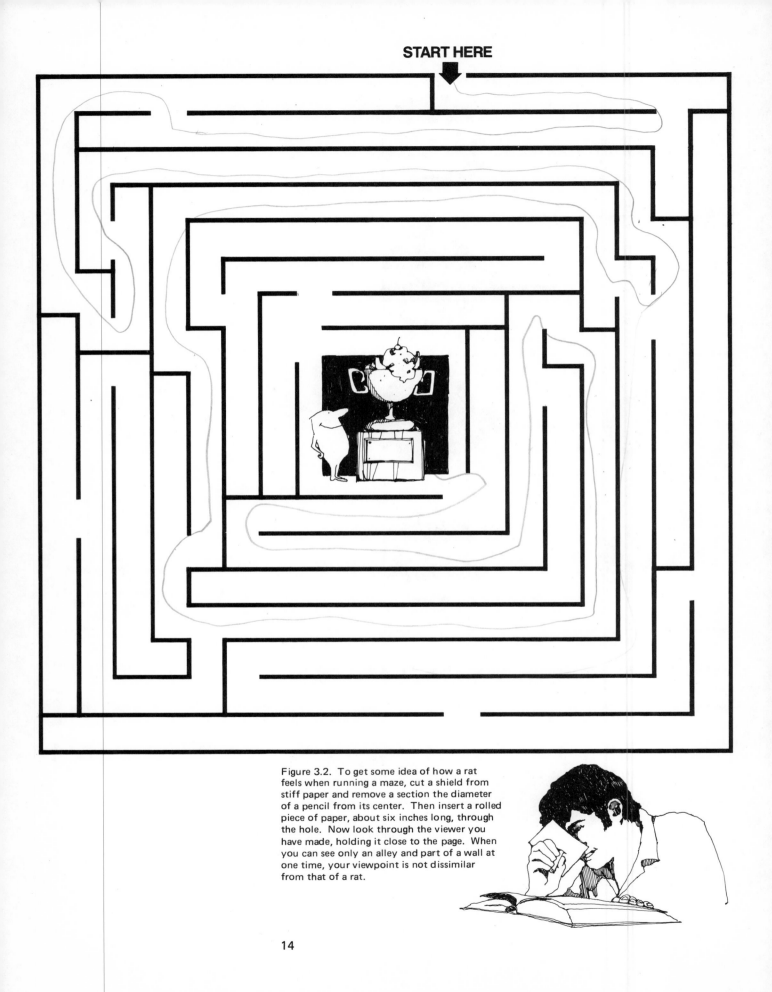

Figure 3.2. To get some idea of how a rat feels when running a maze, cut a shield from stiff paper and remove a section the diameter of a pencil from its center. Then insert a rolled piece of paper, about six inches long, through the hole. Now look through the viewer you have made, holding it close to the page. When you can see only an alley and part of a wall at one time, your viewpoint is not dissimilar from that of a rat.

14

CONCEPT LEARNING

Operant theorists frequently visualize learning as the chaining together of specific responses through reinforcement. How well does this theory answer the following questions?

If you learn to open the door with your right hand, would you need to relearn how to open it with your left?

Can you explain how a creative solution to a problem, a new piece of music, a painting, or an invention comes into being? Can classical conditioning explain these phenomena? Do we depend, in part, upon a higher-order type of learning than classical or operant?

To what use could the principles of classical and operant conditioning be put in changing clinical behavior? Are both types applicable? What type of reinforcer and schedule would you use? Would your solution produce a change in attitudes or just in behavior?

SUGGESTED READINGS

Boring, E. *A History of Experimental Psychology*. New York, Appleton-Century-Crofts, 1950. The definitive book on the history of the various branches of experimental psychology, including both behaviorism and the introspectionist approach.

Hilgard, E. R., and Bower, G. H. *Theories of Learning*. 3rd ed. New York, Appleton-Century-Crofts, 1966. A systematic treatment of major behaviorist theories of learning and also of some non-behaviorist theories.

Honig, W. H. (Ed.). *Operant Behavior: Areas of Research and Application*. New York, Appleton-Century-Crofts, 1966. A collection of papers discussing both recent research and practical applications using Skinner's operant techniques.

Kimble, G. A. *Hilgard and Marquis' Conditioning and Learning*. 2nd ed. New York, Appleton-Century-Crofts, 1961. An excellent summary and discussion of behaviorist research on learning.

Pavlov, I. P. *Conditioned Reflexes*. London, Oxford University Press, 1927. A definitive statement of Pavlov's work, this book is the translation of a series of lectures given in 1924 in which Pavlov summarized his research and theory.

Reynolds, G. S. *A Primer of Operant Conditioning*. Glenview, Ill., Scott, Foresman and Company, 1968. A brief but thorough account of the theory and principles of operant conditioning, as developed from the work of B. F. Skinner and his students.

Skinner, B. F. *The Behavior of Organisms*. New York, Appleton-Century-Crofts, 1961. The book in which Skinner first spelled out his approach to learning.

Skinner, B. F. *Walden Two*. New York, Macmillan, 1948. A novel outlining a utopian society where behavior is programmed according to Skinner's analysis of learning by reinforcement.

Watson, J. *Behaviorism*. New York, Norton, 1930. An introduction to behaviorism by the man who founded it.

4
The Organization of Behavior

David Premack has stated that when two responses are interdependent, the more probable will reinforce the less probable. For example, if a rat is deprived of running (which he normally does), he will *eat* to run. The response (eating, tasting) and not the stimulus (food) is, in this case, the reinforcer. Does this concept of reinforcement make it easier to understand such activities as riding a horse, working a picture puzzle, or going to the moon than does a stimulus explanation? What is the reinforcer in working a nine-to-five job? The answer may be in the concept of chained or secondary reinforcers, whereby the situation allows responses that allow subsequent responses.

REACTING TO THE UNEXPECTED

Expectations are important in our lives. Animals withdraw in fear from unexpected outcomes. People may laugh or cringe at the unusual. Is the theory reasonable that there exists a continuum of reactions to unexpected results, ranging from boredom to fear, as shown below?

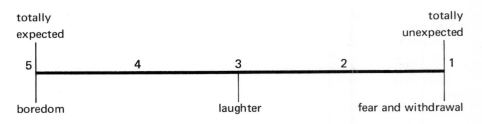

How would you design a simple experiment to test this theory? What controls would you use? What would your independent and dependent variables be?

MAZE BEHAVIOR: RUNNING BLIND OR RUNNING SMART?

Kurt Fischer found that when animals first begin a maze task, they are slow to leave the start box but run faster after they have gotten a start. When they have learned it well, they start quickly and run all the way, apparently having learned to anticipate the reward that awaits them at the goal. An alternative view is that behavior is a chaining together of the individual responses (small motions) that make it up; moreover, that the chain is strongest near the reinforcement. In other words, the chain is weaker at the beginning of the alley and stronger at the end, causing the animal to start slowly and pick up speed as he nears the goal. Finally, all the links in the chain become stronger, all the way back to the starting box.

The first of these explanations is mentalistic or cognitive; the other is atomistic, mechanistic, or associationistic, as it has been variously called. How would you choose between these viewpoints?

The degree to which an animal's response to reinforcement is based on conscious anticipation of the reward was a major issue in psychology during the 1950s. How would the fact that a thoroughly trained rat "voluntarily" runs the maze, even when prefed, influence your conclusion? How about the fact that the animal will stop at a food cup in the middle of the maze, eat, and then continue to run, thereby demonstrating flexibility?

No matter how clever cognitive-oriented explanations become, more sophisticated chaining mechanisms (accounting for flexibility) can always be posited. Efforts to prove that maze behavior is exclusively mentalistic *or* entirely mechanistic have been unsuccessful, despite the volumes of data and analysis this debate has generated. Was the whole debate worthless? The violent disagreements that have raged among psychologists over this issue *have* led to many interesting conclusions about the relationship between input (doing something to a subject) and output (his response).

CUMULATIVE EFFECTS OF OVERLEARNING

Test the theory that underlearned tasks result in negative transfer, whereas overlearned tasks result in positive transfer. Obtain four subjects, or join with your classmates in testing two subjects each. Have half the subjects study List 1 below until they can recall about 50 percent of the items (undertraining). Then see how long it takes them to learn List 2. Let the other half learn List 1 very thoroughly (overtraining) before asking them to learn List 2. Was the second list faster to learn for subjects who were overtrained on List 1? Could there be an alternative explanation of what happened? How would you rule out any alternatives? Was the difference you obtained any greater than the "noise" in the data (variation among subjects) would account for?

List 1	List 2
HPF	JPV
IPW	MPA
NPE	BPC
GPS	XPO
GAW	DAP
FAC	HAZ

SUGGESTED READINGS

Fischer, K. W. *The Organization of Simple Learning.* Chicago, Markham Press (in press). This book presents the research and theory underlying the analysis of learning in terms of phases in the development of an action.

Hebb, D. O. *The Organization of Behavior: A Neurophysiological Theory.* New York, Wiley, 1949. The classic book that helped to cause the resurgence of interest in the organization of behavior in American psychology.

Hebb, D. O., and Thompson, W. R. "The Social Significance of Animal Studies," in G. Lindzey (Ed.), *Handbook of Social Psychology.* Reading, Mass., Addison-Wesley, Vol. II, 1968, pp. 729-774. This paper examines the social implications of some of Hebb's work, including his investigations of the causes of irrational fear.

Premack, D. "Reinforcement Theory," in D. Levine (Ed.), *Nebraska Symposium on Motivation.* Lincoln, University of Nebraska Press, 1965, pp. 123-180. Premack presents his theory of reinforcement and summarizes the data that led to his theory.

UNIT II
Human Development

5 & 6
Development of Intelligence

Heinz Werner advanced the hypothesis that culturally primitive people all think at a preoperational level. If this hypothesis is true, what does it imply about the importance of assimilation and accommodation in obtaining higher levels of thinking? Do you think humans can systematically train themselves to achieve even higher levels of thinking than most of us now reach? Would such an achievement require learning more facts (as through drills in Latin) or solving abstract puzzles?

PATTERN PREFERENCES

One of the earliest demonstrations that infants perceive differences among forms was made by R. L. Fantz in his fixation experiments. He would suspend a variety of patterns, including scrambled and nonscrambled faces, above a child in a special viewing apparatus. An observer hidden from the child noted which pattern the child preferred. Fantz found that infants have definite form preferences. Conduct your own fixation experiment to see if your results are comparable to his.

Procedure

Subjects. Choose a subject from your peer group and, if possible, also an adult or a child around age three for developmental comparisons.

Independent Variables. Use the cards on pages 23 to 29. There are two sets: a corner set and a face set. Each card is labeled on the back with a number that indicates either number of corners (corner set) or degree of incongruity (face set).

Method and Dependent Variable. Show each subject a pair of stimulus pictures from the corner set (line and L). Tell him to look at the two pictures as he wishes for fifteen seconds. Tell him when the fifteen seconds are up. Keep track of the number of times he looks at each stimulus in the pair during the fifteen-second period. Continue to show him pairs of pictures from the corner set, tallying as you go. It is best to develop a strategy for presenting all possible combinations that does not use any picture more than twice in a row, or preference responses will be habituated. For example, try this sequence: line-L, ⊔-triangle, square-pentagon, hexagon-line, L-⊔, triangle-square, and so on. It is important to present each stimulus picture in an equal number of pairings. Repeat for the face set.

Analysis

(1) Add up all the looking frequencies for each stimulus picture in the corner set. For example, add up all the times your subject looked at the line. Which corner stimulus was looked at most frequently?

(2) Review the Spearman correlation method on pages xiii-ix. Correlate the frequency of looking that you obtained for each picture with the number of corners (listed on the back of the cards) in the picture.

(3) Repeat the tally procedure for the face set. Again, which stimulus was most frequently looked at?

(4) For each face picture, correlate the frequency of looking with the face ratings on the back of the card. Does looking relate to incongruity of features? Could your results reflect any other variables?

(5) If you used parents or children, compare your results across the developmental levels. Do you find differences? Why do you think you obtained this result?

What can you conclude about form perception and attention from this experiment? What are the drawbacks of the comparison method?

You could have timed how long your subject looked at each picture. Why would this have been difficult? How would you use timing in addition to frequency of looking? Would the time element have changed the validity of the results?

CONSERVATION

Most children can understand conservations of volume, number, and shape by seven years of age. These concepts are not the only ones humans acquire concerning basic physical principles. There are other, equally basic relationships that may not be understood until a later age, such as conservations of energy, matter, and time. Consider the two examples that follow:

If water is added to the right-hand tank in Figure 5-6.1 until level Y is reached, where will the water be in the other tanks connected to it? Even if you know the answer, can you explain this effect? It involves conservation of pressure. Try this question on any children over five years of age.

Cut a 3-by-3 card (by cutting two inches from a 3-by-5 card), put a pin through the center, and insert the pin into a thread spool, as shown in Figure 5-6.2. If you blow as hard as you can on the end of the spool, what happens? Try it. This phenomenon could be called conservation of pressure and velocity, and it is the basic principle by which many machines work, including airplanes.

Figure 5-6.1. If water is added to vessel A until it reaches level Y, at what level will the water be in vessels B, C, and D?

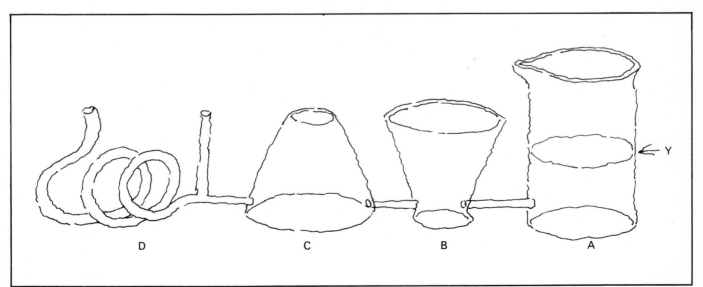

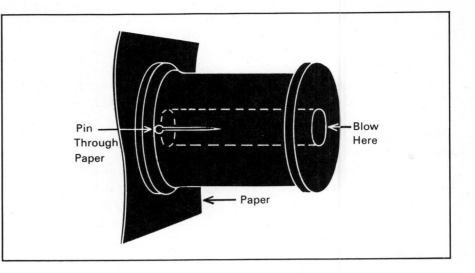

Figure 5-6.2. Arrangement of pin, spool, and cardboard to test "conservation of pressure and velocity."

HOW WE LEARN

Many psychologists (particularly those identified with behaviorist orientations) view learning as a rather atomistic process; elements learned by trial and error are chained by reinforced association into higher-order concepts.

What are the implications for this atomistic explanation of the difficulty of teaching conservation to a child until he is mentally ready for the concept? Does the process of developing different schemes of acting on the environment mean that the process of learning may be different at different stages of development? Does the development of object constancy support the concept of a higher-order chaining of lower-order elements? Where is operant conditioning in Piaget's concepts of assimilation, accommodation, and equilibration?

WHAT IS INTELLIGENCE?

Performance on intelligence tests begins to correlate with later adult mental level when a child is about four years old. Yet, as Piaget has described, the child goes through many transitions in his logical thinking between age four and adulthood. What do you think intelligence tests measure?

SUGGESTED READINGS

Baldwin, A. *Theories of Child Development.* New York, Wiley, 1967. A clear, concise treatment of the major theories of child development, including Piaget's.

Bower, T. G. R. "The Object in the World of the Infant," *Scientific American,* 225 (1971), 30-38. A report of Bower's recent research, in which he has begun to explore the relationship between the infant's advanced perceptual capacities and limited cognitive capacities.

Fischer, K. W. *Piaget's Theory of Learning and Cognitive Development.* Chicago, Markham Press (in press). A clear, easy-to-read summary and discussion of Piaget's theory, with special emphasis on his approach to learning and cognitive development.

Werner, H. *Comparative Psychology of Mental Development.* New York, Science Editions, 1948. A useful compendium of research on mental development, including observations of primitive thought and insanity as well as studies of thought in children.

1

0

3

2

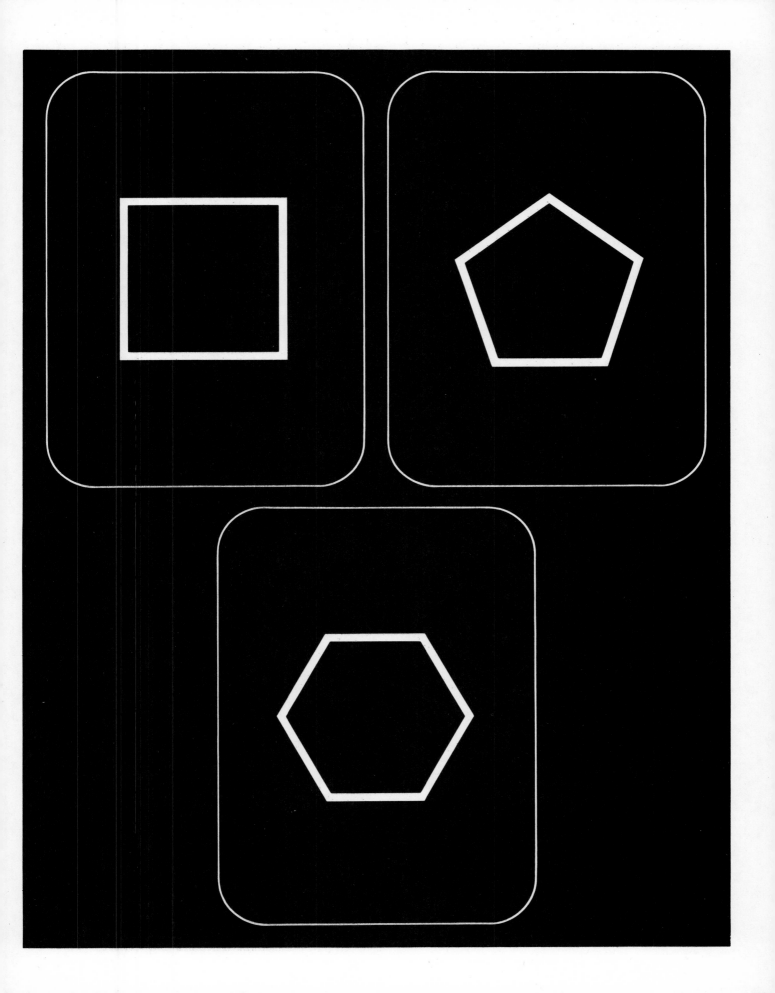

5

4

6

2

NO. PARTS   LOCATION   ORIENTATION
I   C   C

1

NO. PARTS   LOCATION   ORIENTATION
C   C   C

4

NO. PARTS   LOCATION   ORIENTATION
C   C   I

3

NO. PARTS   LOCATION   ORIENTATION
C   I   C

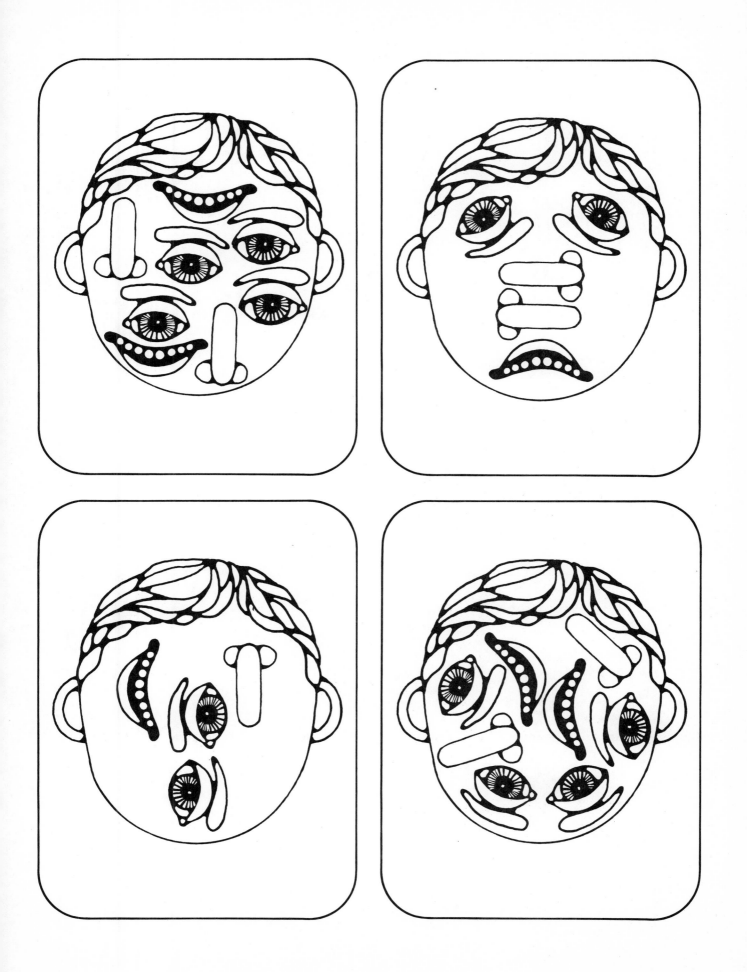

6

NO. PARTS	LOCATION	ORIENTATION
I	C	I

5

NO. PARTS	LOCATION	ORIENTATION
I	I	C

8

NO. PARTS	LOCATION	ORIENTATION
I	I	I

7

NO. PARTS	LOCATION	ORIENTATION
C	I	I

The role of language in thought has been a subject of controversy for many years. Try to do the following problems without implicit speech (talking to yourself).

(1) Mary is twice as old as Henry. Henry is one-and-a-half times as old as George. George is eighteen years old. How old is Mary?

(2) If you have one measuring cup containing one gallon of water and one containing a pint, how can you measure out one quart of water?

(3) What is the next number in the series 1, 25, 2, 16, 3, 9, 4, 4, 5,. . .?

(4) How much implicit thought is required for the problem in Figure 7.1 below?

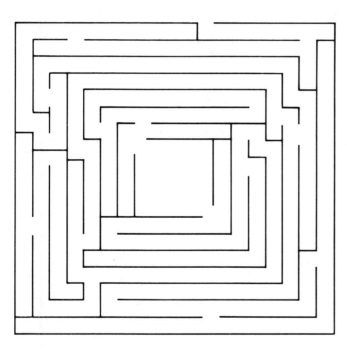

Figure 7.1. How much implicit thought is required to trace the correct path into the center of the maze?

(5) Find the word "frog" as fast as you can:

TOAD	HIDE	MOAT	BOAT
SIDE	FIND	DOLL	BEEN
TEST	THAT	FROG	GOOD
SEEK	ROTE	HAVE	THEY

(6) Tie your shoelaces. Do you use verbal thought? Try to describe to someone verbally (without moving your hands) how to tie his shoelaces. Could you think about it verbally even if you wanted to?

Do there seem to be some mental problems that require implicit verbalization and others that do not? If so, what type of problems falls into each category? Because animals do not verbalize their thoughts, what type of problems are they restricted to?

7
Development of Language

COMPLETING TAG QUESTIONS

Try to supply the tags for the following sentences and, at the same time, to work out the grammatical processes involved.

Pronominalization

That man was here, _____ ?

The boys are playing, _____ ?

The girl is running, _____ ?

The chair tipped over, _____ ?

Both of them did it, _____ ?

The two of us want some, _____ ?

John and Bill went together, _____ ?

John and I went there, _____ ?

John and you went there, _____ ?

Location of Auxiliary Verb

They'll help you, _____ ?

They can help you, _____ ?

They jump rope well, _____ ?

They jumped rope well, _____ ?

He jumps rope well, _____ ?

John's tired, _____ ?

John's finished his lunch, _____ ?

They could have done it, _____ ?

He should have been here by now, _____ ?

Subject of Imperative

Help yourselves, _____ ?

Sit down, _____ ?

Negative-to-Affirmative Alteration

He won't do it, _____ ?

He can't do it, _____ ?

He isn't doing it, _____ ?

He didn't do it, _____ ?

He is happy, _____ ?

He is unhappy, _____ ?

He is not happy, _____ ?

MONKEY TALK

A chimpanzee named Sarah has been taught to use language by psychologist David Premack of the University of California at Santa Barbara. Although her vocal cords cannot produce speech, she can construct sentences using about 130 plastic symbols that stand for things, actions, names, and ideas. Sarah has illustrated her knowledge of syntax by creating sentences with proper word order and rejecting malformed sentences. She understands positive and negative, can make value judgments (based on Premack's likes and dislikes), and can even understand conditional (if-then) statements. What implications does this experiment have for our present definition of language and language learning? Does it suggest that monkeys can develop cognitively?

LAB RAT LIBERATION

Man has prided himself on differing from animals in possessing the highest order of language ability. Washoe and Sarah have given us the first concrete evidence that, although it did not develop spontaneously, monkeys and perhaps other animals can use grammatical rules to combine words in meaningful ways. Experiments are currently underway to see if large colonies of monkeys will commmunicate with signs to each other and if a mother will teach her children signs. Assuming for a moment that such experiments are successful, will the man-animal distinction grow so tenuous that we will have to reconsider our (ab) use of higher-order animals for physiological experimentation? That is, if our sense of ethics prevents our drilling holes into the heads of mental retardates, how will we justify drilling into the heads of chimps, whose mental equipment may be comparable to that of many human retardates?

SUGGESTED READINGS

Bar-Adon, Aaron, and Werner, Leopold. *Child Language: A Book of Readings*. Englewood Cliffs, N. J., Prentice-Hall, 1971. Very valuable collection of papers on all aspects of language development. Gives a historical perspective on the study of language and makes available many previously untranslated papers.

Brown, Roger. *Psycholinguistics*. New York, Free Press, 1970. A compilation of the major papers of Brown and his associates on child and adult language.

Brown, Roger. *A First Language: The Early Stages*. Cambridge, Mass., Harvard University Press (in press). An excellent, comprehensive, and thoughtful identification of the present theoretical issues in early child language learning. Discusses extensively the notion of semantic and grammatical relationships, alternate grammatical descriptions, and the determinants of the order of rule learning in young children.

Cazden, Courtney. "Subcultural Differences in Child Language: An Inter-disciplinary Review," *Merrill-Palmer Quarterly,* 12 (1966), 185-219. An excellent discussion of environmental influences on language development, including the topics of social-class differences and the evaluation of Black Non-Standard English. Useful bibliography.

Chomsky, Carol. *The Acquisition of Syntax in Children from 5 to 10*. Cambridge, Mass., M.I.T. Press, 1969. A report on her investigations into some later aspects of language development, particularly the mastery of more complex syntactic structures.

Chomsky, Noam. *Language and Mind*. New York, Harcourt, Brace, Jovanovich, 1968. A good discussion of a linguist's view of language and mind, as well as a general introduction to Chomsky's system of describing language (transformational grammar).

Furth, Hans. *Thinking Without Language*. New York, Free Press, 1966. Thoughtful discussion of the problem of the relationship of language and thought, based in part on his experiments with deaf children.

8

Social Development: The Case of Morality

It is often useful in understanding psychological phenomena to simplify complex data by sorting them into a manageable number of dimensions. At least three theories of moral development have evolved: A Freudian view, in which guilt lays the basis for moral standards; a social viewpoint, in which social rewards and punishments as well as modeling are important; and, finally, a cognitive-developmental approach suggested by Lawrence Kohlberg, in which advanced levels of moral decisions are based on complex judgments appropriate to each situation.

Rate each of the following deviant behaviors on one of the three scales in Figure 8.1. Some behaviors may fit all scales; in such cases, place the behavior on the most *appropriate* scale. To fit an item on the two-dimensional scales of "Social View" and "Judgmental," find the point you want on one of the two lines, then measure over to the point parallel with the desired value on the other line, as illustrated at the top of page 35.

(1) abortion
(2) adultery
(3) arson
(4) assault and battery
(5) bootlegging
(6) burglary
(7) counterfeiting
(8) embezzlement
(9) forgery
(10) homicide
(11) kidnapping
(12) larceny
(13) libel
(14) perjury
(15) rape
(16) receiving stolen goods
(17) smoking marijuana
(18) smuggling
(19) vagrancy

(20) cheating
(21) incest
(22) homosexuality
(23) withholding income tax because you do not agree with what the government spends it on
(24) mercy killing
(25) sitdown to protest a cause
(26) not returning excess change to a machine or salesperson
(27) bombing residential areas for ideological reasons
(28) voyeurism
(29) killing an animal for the joy of killing
(30) hunting for trophies
(31) selling hard drugs
(32) using hard drugs
(33) buying cigarettes when underage
(34) drunk driving
(35) distributing pornographic materials

Do your scalings help you decide whether or not any one theory is most useful? Or is more than one theory needed to understand the varieties of deviant behavior? Can you think of a scale on which you could locate all thirty-five behaviors?

RELATIVISTIC VERSUS ABSOLUTE MORALITY

Do you support a relativistic view of morality? If morality is not situational and culturally specific, why is it a crime to kill a person during peacetime but not a crime to kill someone on the battlefield? Why do many people insist that killing helpless children is criminal under *any* circumstances?

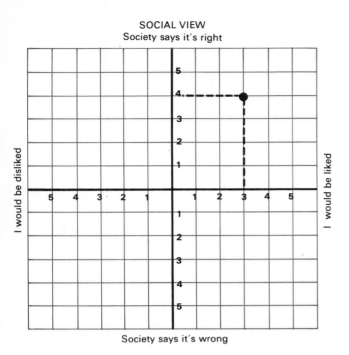

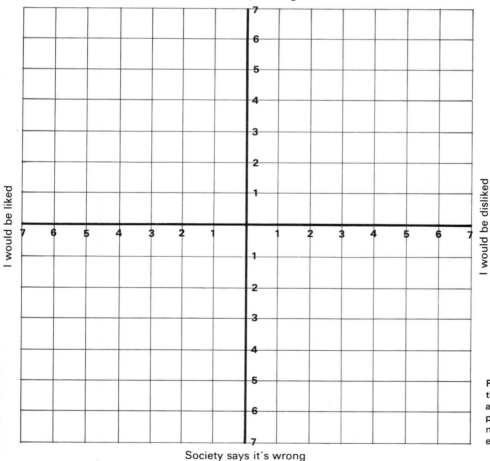

Figure 8.1. Use these three scales on this and the following two pages to find the basis of any moral action according to a social approach (social view), Freudian theory (internal guilt), or a cognitive-developmental explanation (judgmental).

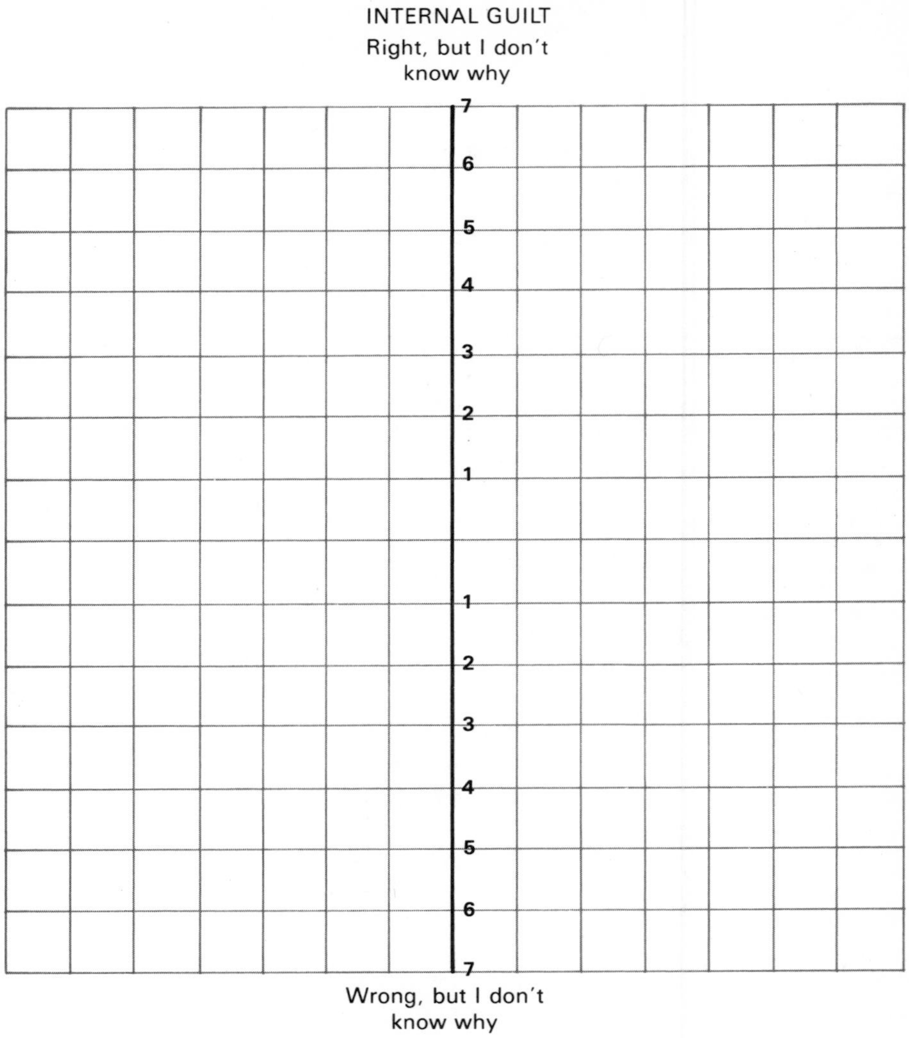

INTERNAL GUILT
Right, but I don't
know why

7
6
5
4
3
2
1

1
2
3
4
5
6
7

Wrong, but I don't
know why

RESPONSIBILITY

What responsibility, if any, has a graduate of a public college to the state, which supplied him with a free education? Do you agree with the motto, "If you have abilities, you have responsibilities," used by Vista (Volunteers in Service to America)?

Suppose a strange disease erased all memories of moral codes from all peoples of the earth, with the exception of yourself. You are, consequently, appointed to retrain everyone else. What kind of morality would you give the world? Would it be based on principles or commands? Would you recommend there be police to enforce the moral codes?

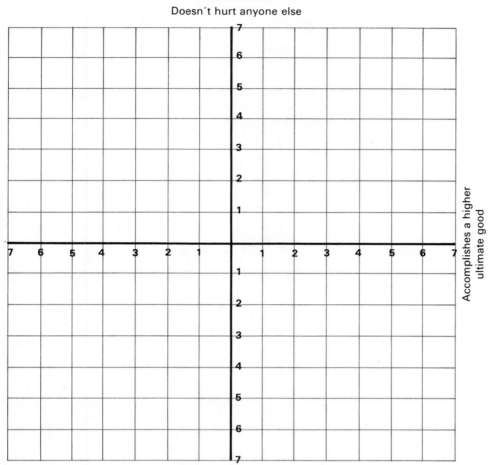

SUGGESTED READINGS

Brown, Roger. *Social Psychology.* New York, Free Press, 1967. Brown's chapter on the acquisition of morality presents an eloquently clear outline of the psychoanalytic, learning-theory, and cognitive-developmental theories of morality.

Freud, Sigmund. Lecture XXXI of the New Introductory Lectures: "Dissection of the Psychical Personality," in *The Complete Works of Sigmund Freud.* Vol. XXII. London, Hogarth Press, 1964, pp. 57-80. This article is the one that deals most explicitly with Freud's view of morality. Other articles are "The Ego and the Id" and "The Dissolution of the Oedipus Complex."

Goslan, David A. (Ed.). *Handbook of Socialization Theory and Research.* Chicago, Rand McNally and Co., 1969. Contains three chapters that supply the single best presentation of theories of moral development—chapters by Aronfreed, Bandura, and Kohlberg. The Kohlberg chapter is his single best work and has been characterized as "inspired." It is one of the most stimulating presentations in psychology in the past few years.

Hoffman, Martin. "Moral Development." In Paul H. Mussen (Ed.), *Carmichael's Manual of Child Psychology* (3rd ed.), Vol. II. New York, Wiley, 1970. An extensive and detailed review of the literature on moral development. It presents the cognitive-developmental position, social-learning theory, and psychoanalytic theory, and systematically surveys the tremendous amount of relevant research.

UNIT III
Memory and Problem Solving

9
Information Processing

One way psychologists analyze thinking is by trying to teach (program) computers to solve the problems we solve. Imagine you have access to a computer that can "understand" the following orders:

(1) Add, subtract, divide, multiply.
(2) Repeat.
(3) Save the value of item _____ .
(4) Recall the value of item _____ .
(5) Identify which of two items is larger.
(6) Direct the keyboard and type.
(7) Follow if-then commands.
(8) Create whole numbers by dropping decimals (for example, 2.67 would become 2).

Using the above commands, you could determine whether 20 + (30 χ 50) is larger than 50 χ 100 by programming your computer to follow the procedure below.

Command	Program
(6)	*Read* value on keyboard (you type 20).
(3)	*Store* value (20) as Item 1.
(6)	*Read* keyboard (type 30).
(3)	*Store* as Item 2.
(6)	*Read* keyboard (type 50).
(3)	*Store* as Item 3.
(1)	*Multiply* Item 2 X Item 3.
(3)	*Store* answer as Item 4.
(1)	*Add* Item 1 to Item 4.
(3)	*Store* answer as Item 5.
(6)	*Read* keyboard (type 50).
(3)	*Store* as Item 6.
(6)	*Read* keyboard (type 100).
(3)	*Store* as Item 7.
(1)	*Multiply* Item 7 X Item 6.
(3)	*Store* answer as Item 8.
(5)	Is Item 4 *larger than* Item 8?
(7)	*If* yes, *then* type "Yes."
(7)	*If* no, *then* type "No."

Using these same eight instructions, program your computer to tell whether a number is odd or even. When you have finished, check your program against that below.

Program for Determining Whether a Number is Odd or Even

Command	Program
(6)	*Read* any number (you type whatever number you choose).
(3)	*Store* as Item 1.
(6)	*Read* number (type 5).
(3)	*Store* as Item 2.
(1)	*Divide* Item 1 by Item 2.

(3)	*Store* answer as Item 3.
(8)	Make Item 3 a whole number.
(3)	Store whole number as Item 4.
(5)	Is Item 3 *larger than* Item 4?
(7)	*If* yes, *then* type "odd."
(7)	*If* no, *then* type "even."

Do we go through this kind of mental sequence whenever someone asks us whether a number is odd or even? Does "teaching" the computer this process help you analyze how you think? Explain.

PERCEPTION AS AN INFORMATION PROCESS

Julian Hochberg and Edward McAlister (*Journal of Experimental Psychology,* 46, 1953, 361-364) studied the proportion of time subjects saw each of the configurations in Figure 9.1 as a cube. They added up the number of single-line segments, angles, and points of intersection necessary to see each configuration as two-dimensional. Then they noted the proportion of time out of 100 seconds subjects saw each as a cube rather than a two-dimensional figure. Table 9.1 lists these rates for each cube. From these results, Hochberg and McAlister concluded that the harder it is (the more information it takes) to see the pattern as two-dimensional, the more likely the pattern will be seen as three-dimensional, which apparently takes an average of only about forty units of information.

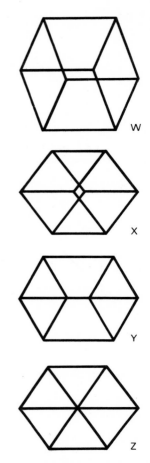

Figure 9.1. Julian Hochberg and Edward McAlister tested subjects to determine what percent of time they saw each of these ambiguous figures as a cube.

	TABLE 9.1				
Figure	% of time seen as cube	No. of lines	Angles	Points of intersection	Total information
W	98.7	16	25	10 =	51
X	99.3	16	25	10 =	51
Y	51.0	13	19	8 =	40
Z	40.0	12	17	7 =	36

Table 9.1. Percentages of time Hochberg and McAlister's subjects saw each of the figures in Figure 9.1 as a cube.

Test this principle, using the four cubes on page 42.   If the principle is correct, one or the other position of a cube in an ambiguous figure should be progressively easier to see, the simpler the cues (lines). The less ambiguous the cues, then, the greater the proportion of time one of two possible cube positions should be seen.

Limit a subject to 100 seconds for each figure. On a second clock keep track of how many total seconds he sees the figure in one position—for example, position A in Figure 9.2. (You can keep track of time spent on one position by plugging in an electric clock whenever the subject sees the cube in that position while consulting a wristwatch for the 100-second time limit.) What proportion of the time was the figure seen in each position? Keep track of your results in Table 9.2.

Does the principle work? In other words, is it easiest to identify as a cube the configuration that is simplest to interpret?

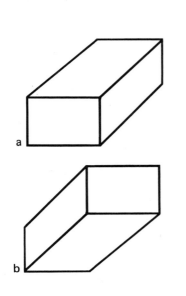

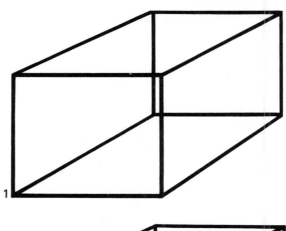

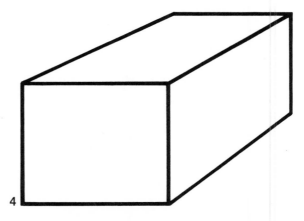

Figure 9.2. Use these four ambiguous figures in your own study of the ease with which each can be seen in one of the two positions identified as (a) and (b).

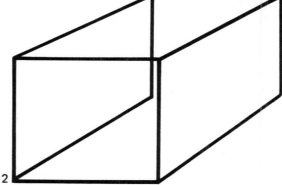

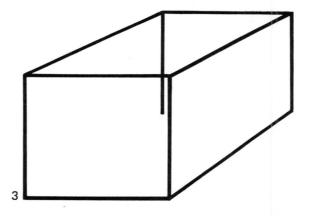

	Percent of 100 Seconds Seen as	
TABLE 9.2		
Figure	a	b
1		
2		
3		
4		

BITS OF INFORMATION

How many bits of information do you need to identify a person's birthday, calculated as month and day? (Answer: four bits for the month and five for the day, totalling nine bits.)

If a letter takes N bits to specify, would the word "quick" take 5 X N bits to specify? (No, because by the time you know q through c, you can probably guess the word.) This illustrates redundancy.

SUGGESTED READINGS

Feigenbaum, E. A., and Feldman, J. (Eds.). *Computers and Thought.* New York, McGraw-Hill, 1963. An early attempt to bring together emerging theories and methods in the simulation of human functions by machines. Contains sections dealing with problem solving, pattern recognition, and question-answering machines.

Miller, G. A. *The Psychology of Communication.* New York, Basic Books, 1967. A good collection of papers. Includes Miller's classic paper, "The Magical Number Seven, Plus or Minus Two: Some Limits on Our Capacities for Processing Information."

Neisser, Ulric. *Cognitive Psychology.* New York, Appleton-Century-Crofts, 1967. An excellent book that draws together a large amount of material relevant to human information processing. Stresses the active, selective, and constructional nature of human intellectual activities, with particularly good treatments of attention, selection, and pattern recognition.

Norman, D. A. *Memory and Attention: An Introduction to Human Information Processing.* New York, Wiley, 1969. The title speaks for itself.

Smith, Frank. *Understanding Reading.* New York, Holt, Rinehart & Winston, 1971. Brings together various lines of research drawn from information processing, physiological psychology, and psycholinguistics and applies them in an understandable and readable form to a familiar topic. Chapters 5 through 11 are particularly relevant.

10
Learning and Memory

Very-short-term memory appears to be visual. To study this type of memory, go into a totally dark room for ten minutes and then flick on a bright light for one second, exposing a newspaper headline. How long after you flick the light off again can you read the print? Does it blur? Is the image replaced or blurred by a second exposure, made shortly after the first?

INTERFERENCE

Memory can be powerfully disrupted by interfering stimuli. Donald Norman of the University of California at San Diego uses this example to illustrate the effects of interference to his students: Say the letters CZB to another person, then *immediately* say the string E,D,T,P,G,C,V. Ask your subject what the first three letters were. Give a different subject KFR followed by E,D,T,P,G,C,V and ask the same question. Did you find that the second string of letters interfered with memory of the first three? Pooling class data on the number of first three letters remembered would be worthwhile.

VISUAL VERSUS AUDITORY MEMORY

Cut out the cards on pages 49-55 and divide them into two stacks—one of pictures, the other of words. You will need two subjects who you can see a week later. Pick ten *words* at random from the list (shuffle cards carefully) and show them to the first subject for one second each. One week later, give the subject the entire deck of words and ask him to pick out the words he saw. Count the number of correct choices (of the original ten) and false identifications. Repeat this procedure with the *pictorial* representations of the words on your second subject. Did your two subjects differ on the percent of correct identifications? Consider when interpreting your results that although it is harder to remember a large amount of information (storage), the more information reviewed during the *search* for the memory (retrieval), the easier is the retrieval. (Pooling class data is recommended.)

MEMORY PEGS

The memory-peg system is a mnemonic device based partly on rhyme. If when you try to remember, the mnemonic does *not* rhyme, you will know you have remembered incorrectly. Also, nouns are more easily visualizable than the numbers they replace.

Teach five of ten subjects the memory pegs on page 46. Then have these five subjects memorize a list of numbers using the memory-peg system. Using the number 10387—hen, tree, gate, heaven—the mnemonic device might be, "There is a hen in the tree by the gate to heaven." Read a series of five numbers to each subject and give him about thirty seconds to process each number in the series. Allow the five people in your control group to have the same amount of time with the numbers.

Test your subjects immediately after they have finished learning each series of numbers. Record the results on the adjacent charts. To test the longevity of the

MEMORY PEGS						
	WITH MEMORY PEGS					
NUMBERS	S$_1$		S$_2$		S$_3$	
	No Delay	24 Hours	No Delay	24 Hours	No Delay	24 Hours
1. 32871						
2. 56418						
3. 50356						
4. 49682						
5. 20917						
6. 17035						

MEMORY PEGS						
	WITH CONTROL GROUP					
NUMBERS	S$_1$		S$_2$		S$_3$	
	No Delay	24 Hours	No Delay	24 Hours	No Delay	24 Hours
1. 32871						
2. 56418						
3. 50356						
4. 49682						
5. 20917						
6. 17035						

memory, contact the subjects, without telling them you are going to do so, twenty-four hours later and ask them to tell you the numbers they memorized.

Memory Pegs

One is a bun.	Six is sticks.
Two is a shoe.	Seven is heaven.
Three is a tree.	Eight is a gate.
Four is a door.	Nine is a line.
Five is a hive.	Ten is a hen.

VISUAL IMAGERY IN MEMORY

Mentally determine where the light switches in your apartment or home are located and keep track of them in your head. Do you have to use visual images to count the switches? To keep track of the number? If not, could you do it with images if you wanted to? Do the methods at your disposal imply different types of memory?

DYNAMIC MEMORY

Memory is not always a static, accurate playback of the original input. Also at work shaping memories are dynamic factors—personal motivations and emotions. Find at least three subjects for this experiment. However, ten or more subjects illustrate the effects of dynamic factors even more dramatically.

You can be the first subject. Look at the following photograph, then write a short description, covering the elements you think a person would remember. Read

this description to your second subject, who has not seen the picture. Let this subject relay the information to still another subject, who has neither seen the picture nor heard the previous transmissions. This chain can be as long as the number of subjects you recruit. Ask the last subject to *write* what he remembers of the message. Compare his description to the beginning version. When Gordon Allport and Leo Postman *(Transactions of the New York Academy of Sciences, Series 2, 8, 1945, 61-81)* applied this procedure to study how rumors develop, they discovered the following effects.

Sharpening.   Certain details are described more carefully than are others.

Leveling.   Unimportant (or uninteresting) details drop out.

Assimilation.   As in confabulation, a person typically changes the message to suit his notions, needs, and emotions.

Identify the sharpening, leveling, and assimilation effects in your findings. Where in the process is simple forgetting?

SUGGESTED READINGS

Adams, J. A. *Human Memory.* New York, McGraw-Hill, 1967. A well-organized book with emphasis upon experimental techniques and findings. It is more technical than the other books listed here, but would make a good companion to Hunter's paperback.

Bartlett, S. C. *Remembering: A Study in Experimental and Social Psychology.* New York, Cambridge University Press, 1932. Although forty years old, this book still warrants reading. Explores Bartlett's convictions that remembering is a more or less skillful and active process of reconstruction and interpretation. Many of Bartlett's ideas resurface in such current work as Neisser's *Cognitive Psychology* and *Studies in Cognitive Growth,* by Bruner and colleagues.

Hunter, I. M. L. *Memory.* London, Penguin, 1964. An introduction to the study of human memory that surveys in narrative form a good deal of experimental literature dating back to Ebbinghaus.

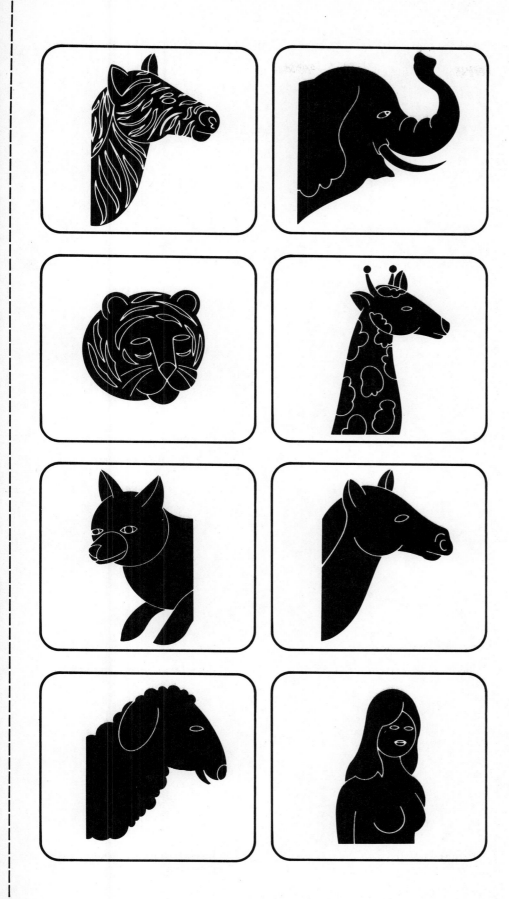

COW	TURKEY	TIGER
GIRAFFE	HORSE	RABBIT
WOMAN	MAN	GOAT
FISH	ZEBRA	ELEPHANT

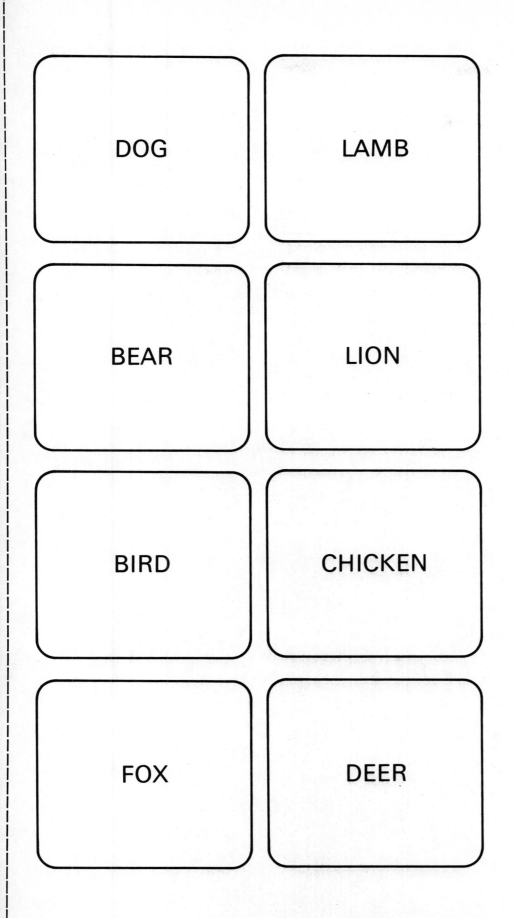

DOG

LAMB

BEAR

LION

BIRD

CHICKEN

FOX

DEER

Some of our habitual ways of solving problems, probably successful in past situations, prevent us from seeing solutions to not-so-typical problems. Try these two problems on another person:

If you wanted to cross a ten-foot moat to reach the island in the center of Figure 11.1, using only two boards (strong enough to walk on) that are each a fraction under ten feet in length, how would you do it? Other aids, such as nails or ropes or pole vaulting, are not permitted. The moat is, for your purposes, bottomless. As your subject works on the problem, can you see him prematurely closing? Figure 11.2 on page 59 shows the solution.

11
Problem Solving

Figure 11.1. Try to cross the ten-foot-wide bottomless moat to the island in the center, using only the two boards, one of which is nine feet, five inches long, the other, nine feet, six inches long. If you are not able to come up with a solution, is it because you prematurely closed? See the solution at the bottom of page 59.

Make a notch (or, preferably, drill a hole) in an unsharpened pencil or smooth round stick. Tie a loop of string on the pencil, as shown in Figure 11.3(a), so that the loop is about one inch shorter than the length of the pencil. Insert the pencil rapidly into someone's shirt buttonhole, as shown in Figure 11.3(b). Pull the pencil through and ask your subject to get the pencil off his shirt. Can you see premature closure in your subject's approach to the problem?

A TEST OF CREATIVITY

How creative are you? Psychologist Sarnoff Mednick developed a test that measures creativity by testing a person's ability to make remote associations. The twenty-item test on page 58 is similar to Mednick's test. A person taking the test is to think of a word that the three given words have in common. For example, the word that "paint," "doll," and "cat" have in common is "house"—"house paint," "dollhouse," and "house cat." After you have taken the test, check your answers against those at the bottom of page 58. You may have discovered another word that links the three given words together that is different from the listed answer.

Foot	(1)	stool	powder	ball
CHEESE	(2)	blue	cake	cottage
	(3)	man	wheel	high
	(4)	motion	poke	down
PARTY	(5)	line	birthday	surprise
PURE	(6)	wood	liquor	luck
GREEN	(7)	house	village	golf
	(8)	card	knee	rope
	(9)	news	doll	tiger
	(10)	painting	bowl	nail
	(11)	weight	wave	house
HAND	(12)	made	cuff	left
STONE	(13)	key	wall	precious
	(14)	bull	tired	hot
	(15)	knife	up	hi
MAN	(16)	handle	hole	police
	(17)	plan	show	walker
	(18)	hop	side	pet
	(19)	bell	tender	iron
BEE	(20)	spelling	line	busy

Ask ten or more people to take the test, or pool your score with those of classmates. Compare the scores. Are art students more creative than math or engineering students? Is a student with an A average more creative than a student with a C average? Are men more creative than women? Does the test, in your opinion, truly measure creativity? Does the ability to free oneself from the traditional modes of solving a problem relate to creativity?

SUGGESTED READINGS

Bruner, J. S., *et al. Studies in Cognitive Growth.* New York, Wiley, 1966. The influence of the different methods of problem representation—in action, image, and symbol—on the problem-solving process are examined in various experimental situations.

Duncan, Carl P. *Thinking: Modern Experimental Studies.* Philadelphia, Lippincott, 1969. Collected readings with a strong methodological bias. Six sections on problem-solving research and six on studies of concept attainment.

Simon, H. A., and Newell, A. "Human Problem Solving: The State of the Theory in 1970," *American Psychologist,* Vol. 26, No. 2, February, 1971. A good, readable statement of the authors' current thoughts on problem-solving research. Includes reference to, and evaluation of, their earlier works, and is therefore a good starting point for anyone interested in detailed study of computer application to the study of heuristic problem solving.

Answers to Creativity Test

(1)	foot	(6)	hard	(11)	light	(16)	man
(2)	cheese	(7)	green	(12)	hand	(17)	floor
(3)	chair	(8)	trick	(13)	stone	(18)	car
(4)	slow	(9)	paper	(14)	dog	(19)	bar
(5)	party	(10)	finger	(15)	jack	(20)	bee

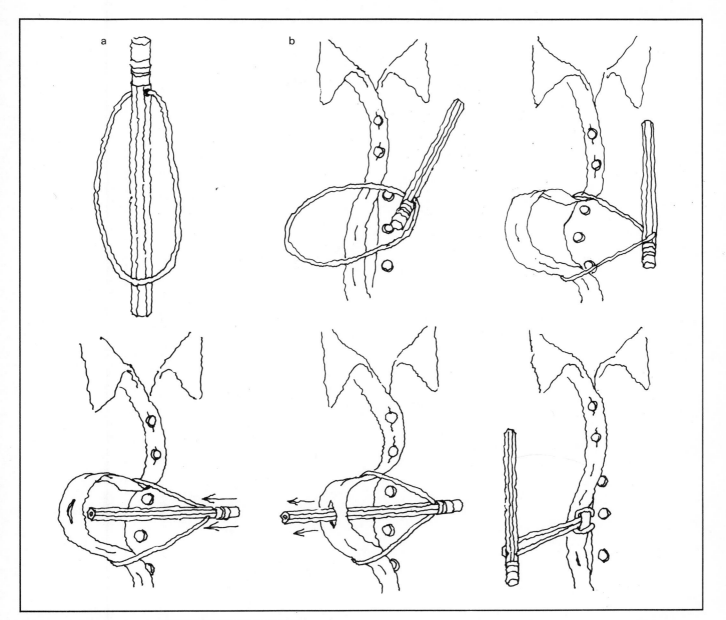

a   b

Figure 11.3. (a) Arrangement of pencil and string to test premature closure in problem solving. (b) Sequence showing how the pencil is inserted and removed. You can expect many subjects to focus on the pencil and string, closing out the distensibility of the shirt as part of the solution.

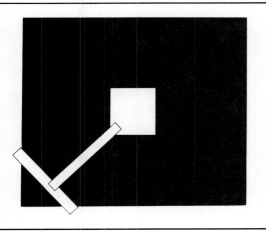

Figure 11.2. Solution to the problem in Figure 11.1.

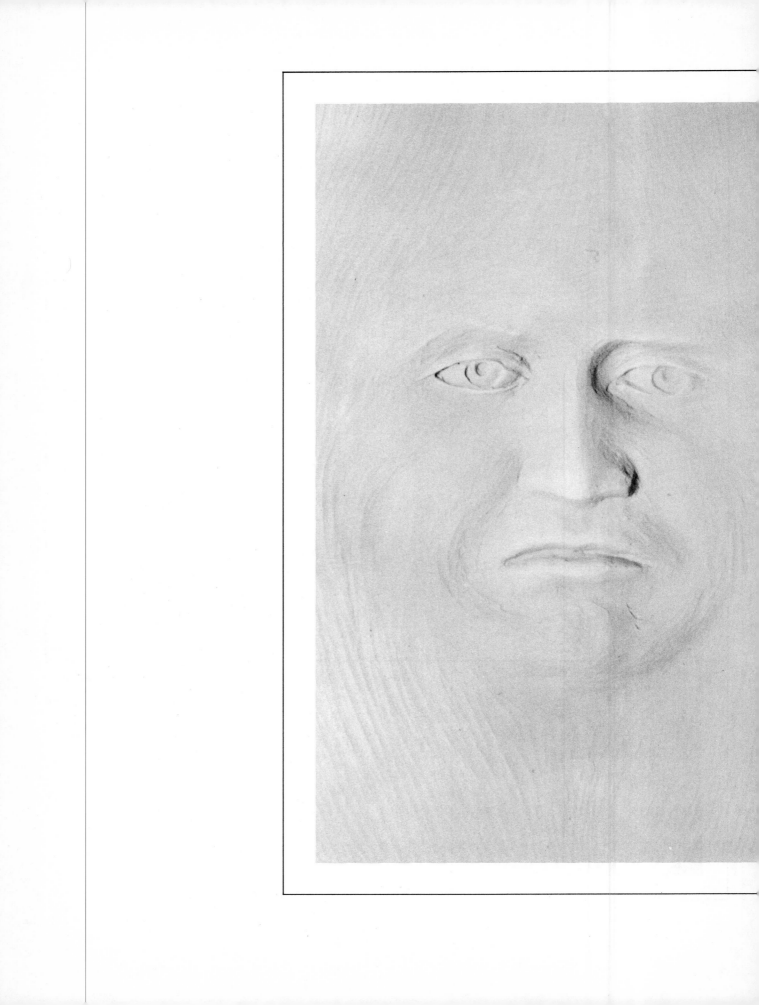

UNIT IV
Perception

12

Sensation and Psychophysics

You are going to determine the threshold distance for resolving the grids on the adjacent page—the distance at which a person can distinguish the stripes. There are several ways of determining threshold distance, so try all the following methods on your subject(s).

(1) *Limits.* Pin up the 90-degree grid. Situate your subject far enough from the grid so that it appears to him to be gray. Have him walk *forward* (no backward steps) until he *just* sees the grid. Measure the distance. It may help to lay down a measuring tape or to mark off distances on the floor—you will be making many measurements around this area. Now have your subject back up until the stripes just disappear; measure. Repeat the whole procedure four more times. Average all ten distances for a single estimate of the threshold.

(2) *Adjustment, or average error.* Leave the 90-degree grid up and ask your subject to move to the spot where he *just* resolves the grid (sees the lines about 50 percent of the time). Measure the distance of this point from the grid.

(3) *Constant stimuli.* Ask your subject to stand, consecutively, just slightly (same distance) to each side of the thresholds measured in (1) and (2). Ask your subject if the grid is resolved at each location (yes or no). Repeat five times at each location (in random order) and calculate the percentage "yes" resolved at each location.

Connect the points in a curve in Figure 12.1 on page 65, as demonstrated below. Draw a line from 50 percent "yes" (if you can) to the curve and connect the other points on the curve with corresponding points along the index. The threshold can be calculated by figuring how far from (2) the arrow points.

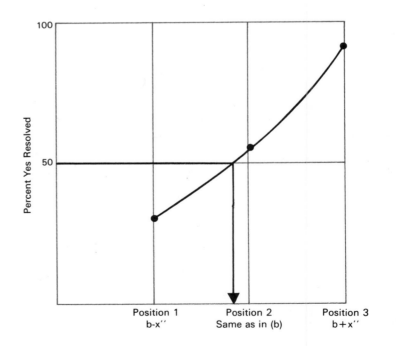

90°

45°

Gray

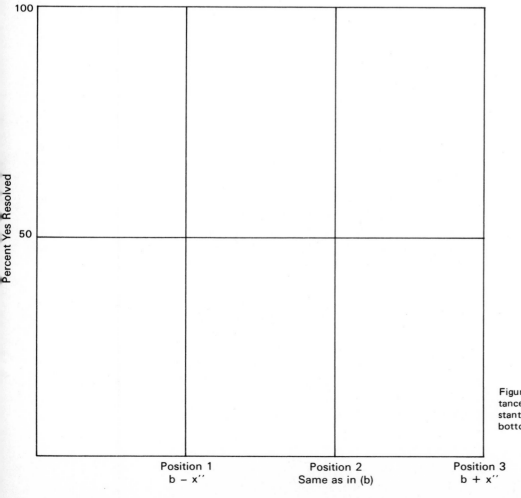

Figure 12.1. Determine the threshold distance from the grids on page 63 by the "constant stimuli" method, as illustrated at the bottom of page 62.

(4) *Signal detection—the two-alternative forced choice.* Pick five distances, locating Position C at about the average of your previous determinations. Positions A and B should be slightly to one side of C with D and E on the other side. (The distances between neighboring positions should be equal.) At each location, show the subject the gray card on one side and a striped card on the other. Have subject tell you which side the stripes are on. Switch them randomly after each choice. Repeat this ten times at each location. Record the number correct at each location, and from this determine the percentage correct. Graph your findings in Figure 12.2. Now, because chance accounts for 50 percent, use the 75-percent level as your criterion. Draw a line from the 75-percent-correct level to the curve connecting the points, then down to the line. The arrow points to the threshold distance.

Were your threshold measurements, obtained with different methods, the same? Which do you have the most faith in, and why?

To determine the role of motivation, repeat (2), but tell the subject it is critical he be *certain* that he can see the stripes. Does his new threshold differ from his old? Would this difference have resulted if signal detection techniques were applied?

For your own interest, use any method to determine whether or not the resolution of a 45-degree grid is the same as of a 90-degree grid.

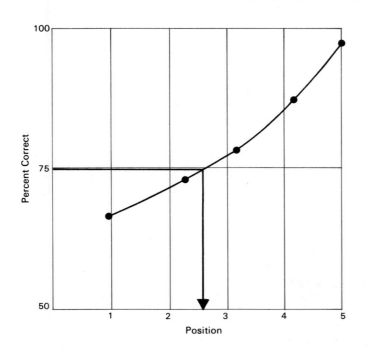

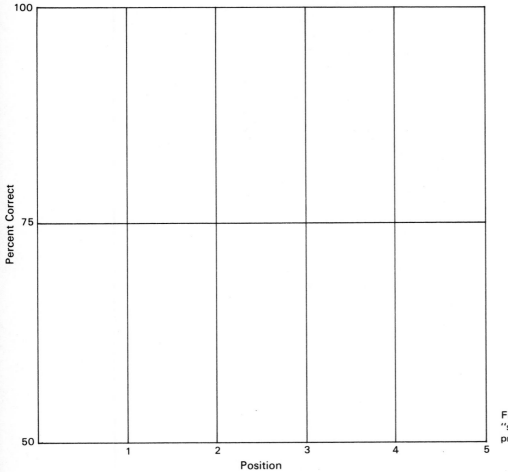

Figure 12.2. Find threshold distance by the "signal detection" method, following the procedure illustrated at the top of this page.

67

THE EYE AS A CAMERA

The eye is often likened to a camera, as shown in Figure 12.3. Discover the differences between the eye and a camera:

The Lens. Look under water. Things should be blurred, because you have many lenses of focus and not just one; water affects the outer one.

Eye Movements. Look at the white dot in Figure 12.4 for twenty seconds, then stare at the black dot. You should see an afterimage moving over the black squares. No matter how hard you try, you cannot make the afterimage steady, because the eye, unlike a camera, is constantly moving.

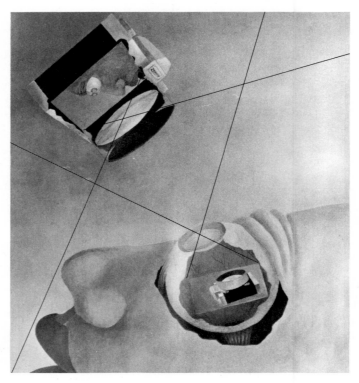

Figure 12.3. The human eye has some features in common with the viewing mechanism of a camera. Notice that the image of each is reversed by the lens of the other.

The Film. Press on the side of your eye; you will see a *phosphene.* Your eye is pressure-sensitive as well as light-sensitive, unlike the film in a camera.

The Fundus. You are looking through a jungle of blood vessels (fundus) all the time. Put a piece of tin foil over a flashlight and poke a 1/8-inch hole in the foil. Go into a dark room for five minutes and shine the flashlight into your eye from an angle, as in Figure 12.5; you should see a pattern of blood vessels similar to that in Figure 12.6. The reason these vessels are not normally seen is that the eye sees only things that move across it; that is why the eye is always in motion. The vessels are part of the eye and move with it.

Storage. Whirl a flashlight around on a string in the dark and you will see a trail. Your film stores the image for awhile, producing what is known as a positive afterimage.

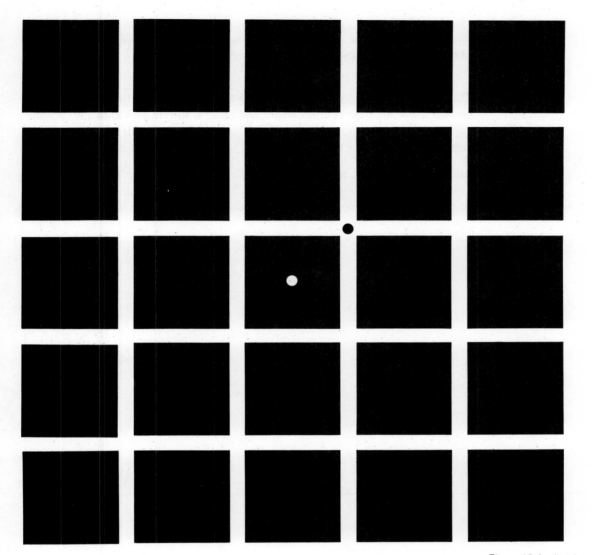

Figure 12.4.   Look at the white dot for twenty seconds, then stare at the black dot. The white lines that appear to move over the black squares are an afterimage.

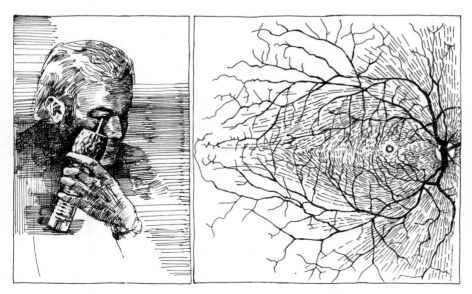

Figure 12.5.   You can see the pattern of blood vessels called the fundus by shining a flashlight at your eye at approximately this angle. You will probably have to experiment some with the angle of the flashlight before the pattern comes into view. For best results, gaze at a blank surface.

Figure 12.6.   The pattern of blood vessels called the fundus, which you can see by following the procedure illustrated in Figure 12.5.

Mosaic. Your "film" is not smooth, but a mosaic of hexagonal receptor cells; under enlargement, the retina looks like a honeycomb. As you should have found in the last problem, a vertical grid is easier to resolve than a 45-degree grid—this results from the mosaic.

The blind spot. Shut your left eye and keep your right eye focused on the "+" below. Hold the page at arm's length and move it toward you until the "X" disappears. There is a hole in your film, which fails to record details about five to eight inches from your face.

Inhibition. Your film has another peculiarity; it suppresses steady, blurred objects. Cast a blurred shadow with a *moving* pencil; it should be so faint you barely see it. Now hold the pencil steady; the shadow should vanish.

SUGGESTED READINGS

Boring, E. G. *Sensation and Perception in the History of Experimental Psychology.* New York, Appleton-Century-Crofts, 1942. One of the finest books in all of psychology. Essential for a historical appreciation of sensation and psychophysics. The book is especially noteworthy for its treatment of the attributes of sensation and the historical antecedents of modern color theory.

Geldard, F. A. *The Human Senses.* New York, Wiley, 1953. Although somewhat dated, this overview of the human senses is one of the clearest accounts in the field.

Green, D. M., and Swets, J. A. *Signal Detection Theory and Psychophysics.* New York, Wiley, 1966. An excellent treatment by the two scientists largely instrumental in developing it. A simpler treatment is contained in Kling and Riggs, cited here.

Judd, D. B. "Basic Correlates of the Visual Stimulus," in *Handbook of Experimental Psychology,* S. S. Stevens (Ed.). New York, Wiley, 1951, pp. 811-867. Judd's treatment of the visual stimulus is still a classic. It is fairly technical, however. For a less technical account, the Geldard book cited here is recommended.

Kling, J. W., and Riggs, L. A. *Woodworth and Schlosberg's Experimental Psychology* (3rd ed.). New York, Holt, Rinehart & Winston, 1971. Includes an excellent and extensive treatment of psychophysics written by Trygg Engen of Brown University. Engen covers basic psychophysical methods, the concept of the threshold, and a detailed analysis of signal detection theory, as well as an extensive treatment of scaling methods.

Go into a totally dark room for ten minutes, then flip on a light for one second, exposing some object. You should experience a strong afterimage. Do colors disappear? Hold your hand out, flip the light on and off again. Now move your hand when the image occurs. Do you experience a conflict?

The Senses

FOVEA VERSUS PERIPHERY

Make a 1/4-inch hole in an opaque card. Look through it, moving your head as you wish. Very little sharp *detail* should be lost, although much of your vision is restricted. Detail is retained because we see sharply only with the tiny central portion (fovea) of our eye. This portion is about as wide as a thumb at arms length.

RECEPTIVE FIELDS

Your visual apparatus, psychologists believe, contains a large number, possibly in the millions, of specialized mechanisms (fields). Each receptive field is sensitive to a separate aspect of vision, such as form, angle, or motion.

Stare at Figure 13.1 (a) on the following page for thirty seconds, then at (b), which should appear to warp.

Try Figure 13.1 (c) for thirty seconds, then (d), which should tilt.

Try (e) for thirty seconds, then (f), which should change spacing.

Cut out the spiral in Figure 13.2 and put it on a turntable (78 rpm, preferably). Look at it for thirty seconds, then at someone's face.

TASTE AND SMELL

Hold your nose and try to taste bread, cheese, milk, or other foods. How much does smell affect taste? Is the effect equal for all foods?

Prepare solutions of salt water (salt), lemon juice (sour), baking soda (bitter), and sugar water (sweet). Dab each solution on your tongue at the points located in Figure 13.3. Where is each taste located?

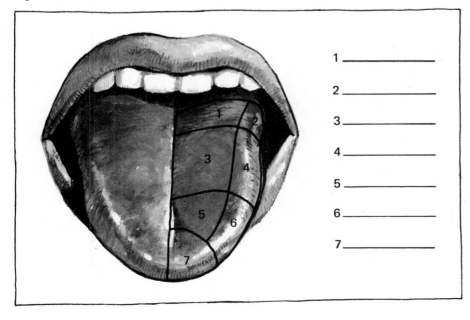

Figure 13.3. Which of these areas of the tongue are sensitive to salt, sour, bitter, and sweet tastes?

1 _____

2 _____

3 _____

4 _____

5 _____

6 _____

7 _____

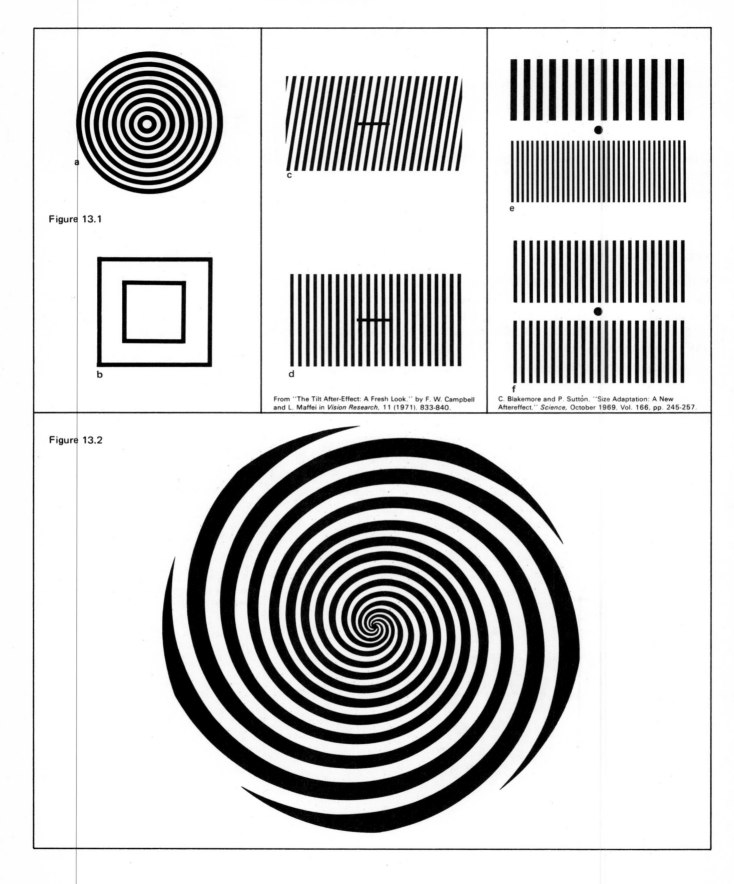

Figure 13.1

From "The Tilt After-Effect: A Fresh Look," by F. W. Campbell and L. Maffei in *Vision Research,* 11 (1971), 833-840.

C. Blakemore and P. Sutton, "Size Adaptation: A New Aftereffect," *Science,* October 1969, Vol. 166, pp. 245-257.

Figure 13.2

VISION VERSUS TOUCH

Write backwards in a mirror:

> your name
> any word
> a spiral

How strongly does vision dominate touch—your kinesthetic sense?

Try the mirror in the two positions shown in Figure 13.4 to see if inversion and left-to-right reversal are equally dominant.

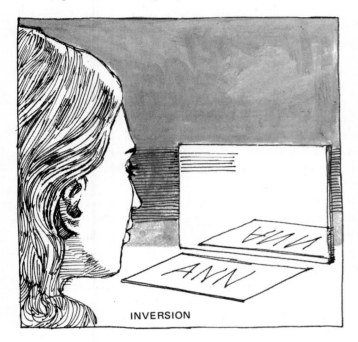

INVERSION

LEFT-TO-RIGHT REVERSAL

Figure 13.4. Place a mirror in each of these two positions, relative to any handwritten or printed material. Which is dominant—inversion or left-to-right reversal?

SUGGESTED READINGS

Boring, E. G. *Sensation and Perception in the History of Experimental Psychology.* New York, Appleton-Century-Crofts, 1942. A marvelous historical introduction to sensation and perception.

Geldard, F. A. *The Human Senses.* New York, Wiley, 1953. Although somewhat dated, this book contains probably the most lucid overview of the human senses available.

Gross, C. G., and Seigler, H. P. (Eds.). *Readings in Physiological Psychology: Neurophysiology/Sensory Processes.* New York, Harper & Row, 1969. Contains many important readings on the processing of sensory information, including work by such giants as Granit, Lettvin, Hernandez-Peon, von Bekesy, and Wald.

Kling, J. W., and Riggs, L. A. *Woodworth and Schlosberg's Experimental Psychology* (3rd ed.). New York, Holt, Rinehart & Winston, 1971. Contains a recent and extensive treatment of the human senses. It includes chapters on the cutaneous senses, the chemical senses, a chapter by Willard Thurlow on audition, and chapters on vision by Riggs, by Boynton (on color vision), and by Alpern (on effector mechanisms in vision).

Teevan, R. C., and Birney, R. D. (Eds.) *Color Vision.* Princeton, N. J., Van Nostrand, 1961. This paperback contains several interesting reprints, ranging from the early writings of Young, Helmholz, and Hering to the pioneer experiments of Edwin Land.

von Bekesy, G. "Hearing Theories and Complex Sounds," *Journal of the Acoustical Society of America,* 35 (1963), 588-601. "Taste Theories and the Chemical Stimulation of Single Papillae," *Journal of Applied Physiology,* 21 (1966), 1–9. *Sensory Inhibition,* Princeton, N. J., Princeton University Press, 1967. These articles by the Nobel-prize winner describe his pioneer work in hearing and taste and with the phenomenon of sensory inhibition.

14
Perception

Perception is a process of construction. Each of us uses his past experiences to interpret (perceive) what his senses have input to his brain.

AMES ROOM

Construct the room as explained in Figure 14.1 inserted after page 80. This room was devised by Adelbert Ames. Look through the viewing port. The room should look normal inside; can you see why? Dangle a penny in each window, using a couple of strands of black thread. You should see, when looking through the viewing port, that one penny appears much larger than the other. What does this tell you about the weight our perceptual system gives to seeing correct room shape as opposed to seeing correct size?

EMMERT'S LAW

We continuously make perceptual judgments like those in the Ames room project. Your perceptual system often sees discrepant information and, therefore, must decide which information it will accept; it does so on the basis of past experience. The Ames room experiment illustrates a preference for one set of visual information over another.

Another example of this weighting phenomenon is the increase in size of the moon on the horizon. Because it appears to us that the low moon is beyond the horizon and a high moon is closer to us than the horizon, the low moon appears larger than the high moon. Emmert's law is still another interesting example. Stare for thirty seconds at the stimulus in Figure 14.2. Now fixate on a distant white wall. An afterimage of the figure should be visible, and its apparent size should be much larger than the original stimulus. Try the experiment again, but this time fixate on a very near surface; the size should shrink, because your perceptual system is calculating the size on the basis of a perceived distance estimate.

Figure 14.2. Fix your eyes on the cross hairs within the star for thirty seconds. Then stare fixedly at a distant white wall. You should see an afterimage that appears to be much larger than this stimulus.

VISUAL DISCRIMINATION

You can see another illustration of perceptual learning if you slowly back away from Figure 14.3. At some point, you should be able to identify the figure; the dot clusters may appear to rearrange suddenly. You have re-sorted the dots on the basis of the pattern you are beginning to recognize. Beyond this distance, gray tones should develop—the resolution of the eye can no longer separate the dots, and they are blended.

Figure 14.3. Prop this figure up against something or have someone hold it as you slowly back away from it. Perceptual learning should take place rather suddenly.

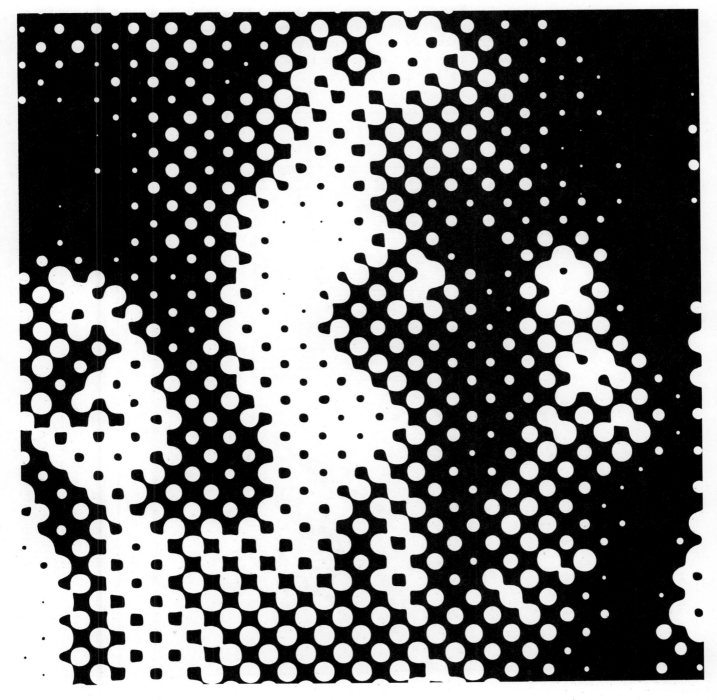

COLOR CONSTANCY

Your visual system tries to keep colors the same no matter what color illuminates them. One consequence of this tendency can be seen in the following demonstration: Shine a white light and a red light on a piece of paper. The paper should appear pink. Now block the red light; what color is the shadow?

BRIGHTNESS CONSTANCY

Figure 14.4. To discover how your visual system tries to hold any object at a constant brightness, punch a hole through a white card and rotate the card so that different brightnesses of light reflect off it. Does the brightness of the hole seem to change when different brightnesses of light are reflecting off the card?

Your visual system also tries to keep objects equally bright no matter how strong the light really is. Demonstrate this effect by punching a hole in a white card. Look through the hole when little light is reflecting on the card. Rotate the card to pick up more light, as shown in Figure 14.4; what happens to the darkness of the hole? You have fooled your eyes.

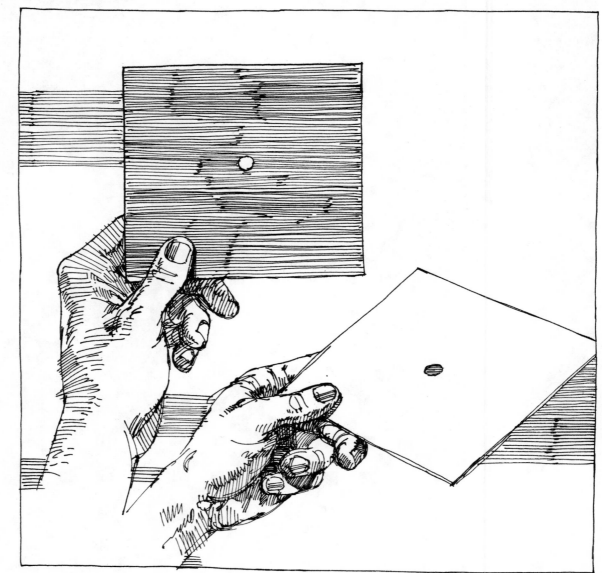

SENSORY ADAPTATION

Write while looking only at a mirror until it begins to feel natural. Then write normally. Does normal writing now feel strange?

THE PULFRIC EFFECT

The ability of our eyes to turn in or out in order to fixate on an object is called *convergence*. Signals obtained from muscle position during convergence are a primary means of determining depth. You can demonstrate this relationship through the Pulfric effect. Make a pendulum that swings over a pencil or other thin, stationary object in a straight arc, as shown in Figure 14.5(a). Look at the weight on the pendulum; it should appear to be oscillating over the top of the pencil. Now hold one lens from a pair of nonprescription sunglasses (or other dark glass) in front of one eye. This lens will slow the message of that eye to the brain and give false information about the object-muscle position relationship. The weight should now appear to make an elliptical arc around the pencil, as shown in Figure 14.5(b).

SATIATION

Gestalt theory assumes that the higher-order perception areas in the brain can be fatigued by a constant input. Stare at the ambiguous Figure 14.6 for sixty seconds. Try to stop it from reversing. Can you? Or does it reverse whenever some level of satiation appears to have been reached?

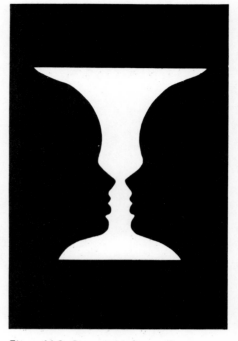

Figure 14.6. Stare at this figure. Can you force yourself to see only *one* of the two possible interpretations?

Figure 14.5. The Pulfric effect. (a) The pendulum, which you can make with a string tied around any sufficiently heavy small object—like a ring—appears to the naked eye to be swinging in an arc over the top of the pencil. (b) With a piece of dark glass in front of one eye, the pendulum weight appears to move around the pencil in an elliptical pattern.

SUGGESTED READINGS

Beardslee, D. C., and Wertheimer, M. (Eds.). *Readings in Perception.* New York, Van Nostrand Reinhold, 1958. An excellent and broad collection of readings including many classical perceptual studies.

Boring, E. G. *Sensation and Perception in the History of Experimental Psychology.* New York, Appleton-Century-Crofts, 1942. A classic and often facinating coverage of the history of sensation and perception.

Droscher, V. B. *The Magic of the Senses: New Discoveries in Animal Perception.* New York, Harper & Row, 1971. Introduces the fascinating world of animal perception.

Gibson, E. J. *Principles of Perceptual Learning and Development.* New York, Appleton-Century-Crofts, 1969. A fine treatment of perception, stressing learning and developmental aspects.

Gibson, J. J. *The Senses Considered as Perceptual Systems.* Boston, Houghton Mifflin, 1966. An excellent treatment of the dependence of perception upon stimulation.

Gregory, R. L. *The Intelligent Eye.* New York, McGraw-Hill, 1970. Gregory stresses his view that perception is a set of simple hypotheses about reality that depend upon sensory experience. The book is particularly strong on visual illusions.

Hochberg, J. E. *Perception.* Englewood Cliffs, N. J., Prentice-Hall, 1964. A good general treatment of perception in paperback.

Hurvich, L. M., and Jameson, D. *The Perception of Brightness and Darkness.* Boston, Allyn & Bacon, 1966. An excellent treatment of our perception of brightness and darkness.

Kohler, W. *Gestalt Psychology.* 2nd ed. New York, Liveright, 1947. Kohler stresses the classical Gestalt approach to perception.

Spigel, I. M. (Ed.) *Readings in the Study of Visually Produced Movement.* New York, Harper & Row, 1965. A book of readings on the perception of movement.

Uhr, L. (Ed.). *Pattern Recognition: Theory, Experiment, Computer Simulation, and Dynamic Models of Form Perception and Discovery.* New York, Wiley, 1966. A book of readings on the sub-area of pattern recognition.

Vernon, M. D. (Ed.). *Experiments in Visual Perception.* Baltimore, Penguin, 1966. Another excellent collection of readings, including reprints of many classical perceptual studies.

We do not sense much of the world. We do not hear air molecules moving randomly, although our hearing is almost this sensitive. We cannot see ultraviolet or radio waves. We cannot taste red, see noise, or feel the solar wind. What, then, is the real reality?

Look closely at a colored comic strip; it is rendered by printing many small dots of colored ink. But any particular color you see at first glance may not contain any dots of that color. Purple, for example, is composed of red and blue dots.

How many odors a dog smells we will never know; nor what the world is like for the sonar navigating bat or the vibration-sensitive spider.

Suppose we saw only changes in brightness, not its absolute amount. The scene in Figure 15.1(a) would look like Figure 15.1(b).

15
Consciousness and Awareness

a

b

Figure 15.1. If humans saw only *changes* in brightness and not its absolute amount, the scene in (a) would look like (b).

HABITUATION AND ATTENTION

Have two people talk to you at once. How good are you at listening to them both? Can one prevent you from listening to the other? To see how particular stimuli affect level of habituation, have one person read Paragraph A (from a sex manual) and another, Paragraph B (from a telephone book).

Paragraph A

Pleasure is the strongest motive for sexual activity. Sexual interest and excitement find their obvious goal in the most intense physical pleasure: orgasm. However, already the increase of excitement before orgasm is experienced as pleasure. It is characteristic of the sexual drive that the desire as well as its fulfillment create pleasurable feelings.

Paragraph B

Nuss, Janet, 3841 Cauby, 243-5874; Nuss, Paul, 546 Fontaine, 245-5893; Nussbaum, Emery I., 7763 Stevens Blvd., 583-7789; Nussbaum, Henry H., 4434 Vista, 273-9477; Nussbaumer, Albert E., 499 14th, 753-4687; Nussey, Eloise, 3323 Indiana, 587-6672; Nussman, Ernest K., 92606 Mariposa, 245-9865.

Which is easier to tune out?

MEDITATION

Stare intently for several minutes at the pattern in Figure 15.2. Concentrate on two aspects: the floating of the form in space and color. Then try concentrating on only one aspect. What did you see? Were outside influences hard to tune out? Did spontaneous thoughts occur during this meditation?

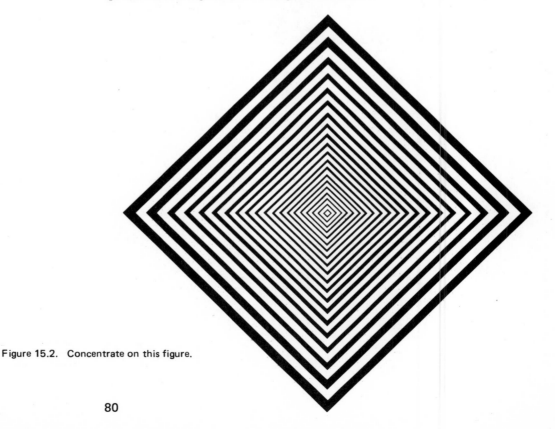

Figure 15.2. Concentrate on this figure.

PERCEIVING TIME

See how accurately a subject can estimate ten seconds and sixty seconds (a) when he is concentrating on the time task, and (b) when he is concentrating on Figure 15.2. Does the sense of time require concentration? Can you hypothesize from this experiment what mechanisms allow us to estimate the passage of time?

THE NEED FOR VARIETY

What do sensory deprivation experiments reveal about the possibility that the need for varied experience is a basic drive, like the needs for food and air?

SUGGESTED READINGS

Dement, W. C. "An Essay on Dreams: The Role of Physiology in Understanding Their Nature." In F. Barron, et al., *New Directions in Psychology*, Vol. II. New York, Holt, Rinehart, and Winston, 1965. A well-written summary of research on the psychology and physiology of dreams by one of the major researchers in the field.

Galton, Francis. *Inquiries into Human Faculty and Its Development.* New York, Everyman, 1911. A fascinating book, originally published in 1883, by one of the greatest psychologists of the nineteenth century. It contains many interesting observations on hallucinations, imagery, and other phenomena relevant to consciousness and awareness.

Gazzaniga, M. S. "The Split Brain in Man." *Scientific American,* 217 (1967), 24–29. A highly readable summary and discussion of the effects of the split-brain operation in man.

Laing, R. D. *The Divided Self.* Baltimore, Penguin, 1965. This well-written book tries to give the reader a sense of what it is like to experience schizophrenia.

Penfield, W. "Consciousness, Memory, and Man's Conditioned Reflexes." In K. H. Pribram (Ed.), *On the Biology of Learning.* New York, Harcourt Brace Jovanovich, 1969. A recent summary of Penfield's research and theory on brain functioning, written especially for nonspecialists.

Shor, R. E., and Orne, M. T. (Eds.). *The Nature of Hypnosis.* New York, Holt, Rinehart and Winston, 1965. This collection of readings contains most of the important papers on hypnosis and also some papers on related topics like multiple personality and spirit possession. The book includes many of the papers discussed in the chapter: those by Thigpen and Cleckley; Pattie; Orne; Erickson; and Hilgard, Hilgard, and Newman.

Sperry, R. W. "A Modified Concept of Consciousness." *Psychological Review,* 76 (1969), 532–536. The famous neuropsychologist argues that consciousness can no longer be viewed as an unscientific concept. Consciousness is held to be a property of the functioning of the brain and plays an active role in the control of brain activity.

Tart, C. T. (Ed.). *Altered States of Consciousness.* New York, Wiley, 1969. This collection of readings includes papers on a wide range of topics, including dreaming, hypnosis, drugs, and meditation. Among the papers are a "fact sheet" on marijuana and many useful papers that are difficult to obtain elsewhere.

Wallace, R. K., and Benson, H. "The Physiology of Meditation," *Scientific American,* 226 (1972), 84–90. This important study demonstrates that meditation has powerful effects on human physiology.

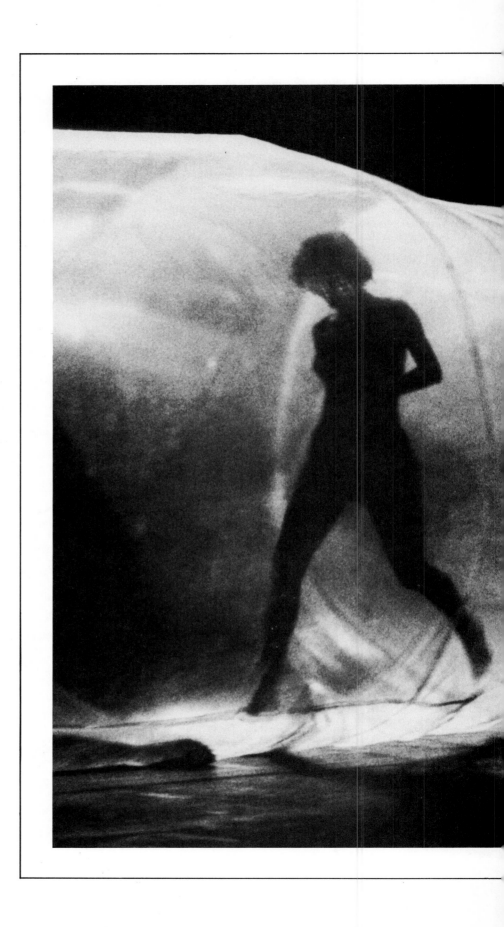

UNIT V
Physiological Bases of Behavior

16 THE BIOLOGICAL ORGANISM

16 The Biological Organism

If psychology is the study of behavior, why do psychologists need to understand how we work physiologically? Or, conversely, if behavior is eventually to be explained physiologically, why do we study psychology?

BRAIN FUNCTION

What problems would arise in trying to derive two brains from one by cutting the corpus callosum? What benefits?

If the brain works by a series of digital all-or-none neural spike discharges and the computer works by all-or-none decisions, can we conclude that the brain is a very compact computer? Where do you think consciousness fits in? If you believe in a soul, where does it reside?

CONSCIOUSNESS

Must an animal be conscious to learn a rule? Simple earthworms can learn rules, but do they possess consciousness? Define consciousness. What does it take for an organism to be conscious?

IMPLICATIONS FOR THE FUTURE

If we could precisely pinpoint the site in the brain of anxiety and hostility (which lies roughly within the hypothalamus), could cutting out this area solve the world's problems and our personal tensions as well? How about removing all emotional centers to enhance the efficiency of the organism?

What do you think about the use of human volunteer subjects in physiological experiments, such as implantation of electrodes in the brain?

REACTION TIME

Each person has a reaction time—that is, a speed of reacting after a signal is given. Thus, one person can step off the curb more quickly than another when the pedestrian signal flashes "Walk." Reaction time is determined by the interaction of the sensory portion of the nervous system with motor activities.

You can measure individual reaction times with a ruler. Have each subject stand in a doorway with the palm of his hand next to the door jamb and his fingers curved around the corner. Take a ruler—a yardstick is best—and hold it flat against the door jamb above his hand so that the zero line is under his middle finger.

Tell him that you are going to drop the ruler and that he is supposed to stop it with his fingers as soon as he sees it start to fall. Let go and then record the distance the ruler fell before he stopped it.

Give each person several practice trials. Five experimental trials should give you enough raw data. You can take the median score as most representative for each subject.

Because an object falls at the rate of 32.2 feet per second, you can calculate a person's reaction time quite accurately. If the ruler fell 6 inches before he stopped it, his reaction time was 0.176 seconds. Table 16.1 can be used to convert distances (inches) into time (seconds).

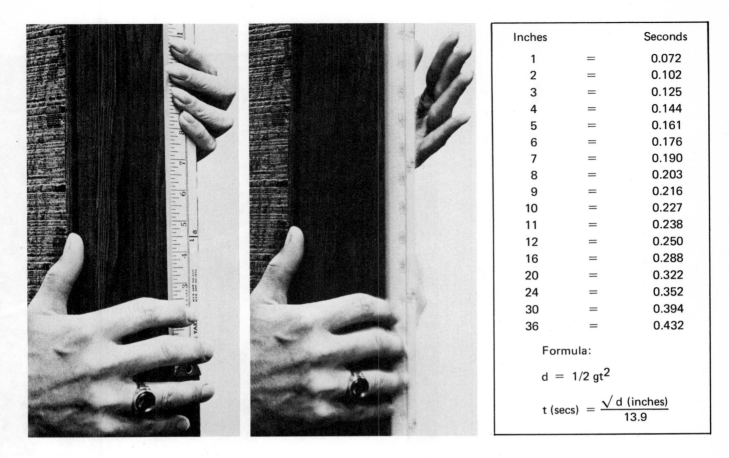

Inches		Seconds
1	=	0.072
2	=	0.102
3	=	0.125
4	=	0.144
5	=	0.161
6	=	0.176
7	=	0.190
8	=	0.203
9	=	0.216
10	=	0.227
11	=	0.238
12	=	0.250
16	=	0.288
20	=	0.322
24	=	0.352
30	=	0.394
36	=	0.432

Formula:

$$d = 1/2 \, gt^2$$

$$t \text{ (secs)} = \frac{\sqrt{d \text{ (inches)}}}{13.9}$$

Does an athlete have a faster reaction time than his girl friend? Are boys faster than girls? Are older people slower? Do alcohol and drugs slow down a person's reaction time? Is a person faster with one hand than the other?

Table 16.1. Convert inches into time when measuring speed of reaction with a yardstick.

SUGGESTED READINGS

Gardner, E. *Fundamentals of Neurology*. 4th ed. Philadelphia, Saunders, 1963. This classic gives an excellent treatment of the anatomy and the physiology of the nervous system.

Gross, C. G., and Zeigler, H. P. *Readings in Physiological Psychology: Neurophysiology/Sensory Processes*. New York, Harper & Row, 1969.

Gross, C. G., and Zeigler, H. P. *Readings in Physiological Psychology: Learning and Memory*. New York, Harper & Row, 1969.

Grossman, S. P. *A Textbook of Physiological Psychology*. New York, Wiley, 1967. A rather extensive treatment, containing over 900 pages.

Katkin, E. S. *Instrumental Autonomic Conditioning*. New York, General Learning Corporation, 1971. This pamphlet gives a good overview of work on instrumental conditioning of autonomic functioning.

Magoun, H. W. *The Waking Brain*. 2nd ed. Springfield, Ill., Charles C. Thomas, 1963. A fascinating treatment of the brain, including the historical antecedents of current work in arousal, attention, and learning.

McGaugh, J. L. (Ed.). *Psychobiology: Behavior from a Biological Perspective*. New York, Academic Press, 1971. This excellent new book provides interesting treatments of several topics of interest, including the evolution of behavior, instinct, sensory processes and behavior, appetitive motivation, attention, and a discussion of brain mechanisms of memory.

Teitelbaum, P. *Physiological Psychology*. Englewood Cliffs, N. J., Prentice-Hall, 1967. This paperback is an excellent overview of physiological psychology; considerably less detailed than the comprehensive text by Grossman, cited above.

UNIT VI
Emotion and Motivation

17 Emotion

THE PROBLEM OF DEFINING EMOTIONS

Before we can investigate emotions, we must define the terms we use. Define each of the following emotions.

fear _____

terror _____

anxiety _____

rage _____

anger _____

hate _____

depression _____

sorrow _____

jealousy _____

shame _____

surprise _____

joy _____

euphoria _____

pride _____

love _____

From this exercise you may discover the difficulty psychologists have in defining their terms. You may have found yourself relying on examples to define the terms above, which is how such terms are usually defined. For example, "Fear is an emotion I feel when I am in danger." We assume that others can understand what we mean by fear because they feel the same emotion when they are in danger. We simply agree to label our emotion when in danger "fear." Psychologists call this type of definition an operational definition.

How do we really know that we all feel fear in the same way? How could we design a simple experiment to find out? Can a person who has never been in danger know what fear is?

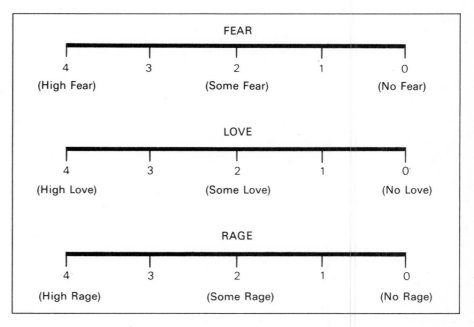

Figure 17.1. The rating scales for ranking various emotions.

TRYING TO QUANTIFY EMOTIONS

J. B. Watson felt that there are three primary emotions—fear, love, and rage—and that all others are derivatives of them.

Make three rating scales for fear, love, and rage, as shown in Figure 17.1. On Chart 17.1, rate each of the fifteen emotions listed above on these three scales. For example, fear would probably rank 3 on fear (because terror would rank 4), 0 on love, and 0 on rage.

Do you find the three scales of fear, love, and rage adequate to describe each emotion fully? If not, what scales would you use? What scale could account for action, arousal, curiosity, and hedonism?

Chart 17.1. Ranking of emotions along the scales shown in Figure 17.1.

EMOTION	RANK														
	Fear					*Love*					*Rage*				
	4	3	2	1	0	4	3	2	1	0	4	3	2	1	0
Fear															
Terror															
Anxiety															
Rage															
Anger															
Hate															
Depression															
Sorrow															
Jealousy															
Shame															
Surprise															
Joy															
Euphoria															
Pride															
Love															

Wilhelm Wundt, on the other hand, posited the following three scales to account for our emotional states:

5	4	3	2	1
pleasantness				unpleasantness

5	4	3	2	1
excitement				quiet

5	4	3	2	1
tension				relaxation

Finally, factor-analytic analysis arrived at these dimensions:

5	4	3	2	1
good				bad

5	4	3	2	1
active				passive

5	4	3	2	1
intense				not intense

Are these scales better than Watson's? Do they depend on the experimenter's values for definition and quantification?

COMMUNICATING EMOTION

Use the masks on pages 91-97 to study the importance of each region of the face in communicating emotions. Try to communicate to another person each of the fifteen emotions listed above, using each of the masks:

eyes only   eyes and mouth only
mouth only   face

Ask a subject to pick out the intended emotion from the list. Because your subject can see the list, your presentations must be selected at random from the list. Score on Chart 17.2, page 99, the number of correct choices he makes for each mask. How important are the eyes, mouth, eyes and mouth, and the rest of the face (whole face minus eyes and mouth) in communicating emotion? Pool your data in class; does a consistent trend emerge?

THE SURVIVAL VALUE OF EMOTIONS

Charles Darwin argued that emotions have survival value. For example, fear immobilizes a person so that he is prevented from continuing a possibly disastrous act. What do you think about Darwin's theory of emotion? Consider the survival values of hate and anger as well as joy and love.

On the following pages are outlined the four masks to be used in testing the contribution of the eyes and mouth in nonverbal communication of emotions. Each of the four masks should be cut out of the book along the dotted line; the entire page comprises the mask. Cut out the pieces outlined and discard them. The masks may be attached to the experimenter's face with tape and/or string.

CUT OUT AND DISCARD

CUT OUT AND DISCARD

CUT OUT AND DISCARD

CUT OUT AND DISCARD

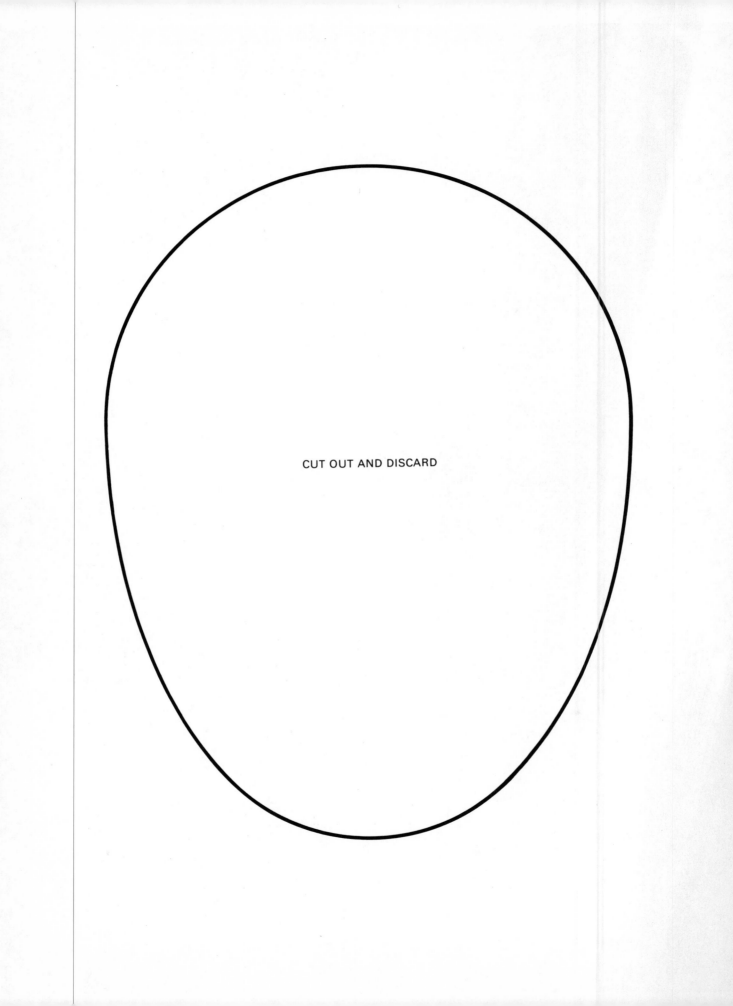

CUT OUT AND DISCARD

EMOTION	MASK				TOTAL
	Eyes	*Mouth*	*Mouth plus Eyes*	*Face*	
Fear					
Terror					
Anxiety					
Rage					
Anger					
Hate					
Depression					
Sorrow					
Jealousy					
Shame					
Surprise					
Joy					
Euphoria					
Pride					
Love					
TOTAL					

Chart 17.2. Scoring matrix for recording *correct* choices in the test of nonverbal communication of emotions.

a

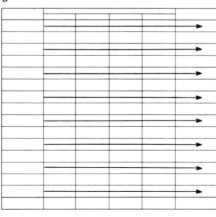

b

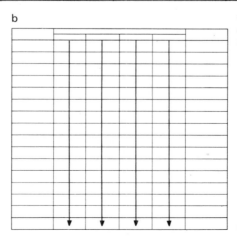
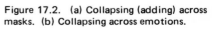

Figure 17.2. (a) Collapsing (adding) across masks. (b) Collapsing across emotions.

SUGGESTED READINGS

Arnold, M. B. *Emotion and Personality.* New York, Columbia University Press, 1960. A two-volume work, the first dealing with the psychological aspects of emotion, the second with the neurological and physiological aspects. Besides being a greatly detailed review it also sets forth Arnold's theory for viewing emotion.

Cannon, W. B. *Bodily Changes in Pain, Hunger, Fear, and Rage.* 2nd ed. New York, Appleton-Century-Crofts, 1929. This work contains Cannon's critical review of the James-Lange theory and presents his alternative theory based on the research that is the major portion of the book.

Darwin, C. *The Expression of the Emotions in Man and Animals.* Chicago, University of Chicago Press, 1965. This classic work, first published in 1872, illustrates and describes the range and method of emotional expression in both animals and man.

Glass, D. C. (Ed.). *Neurophysiology and Emotion.* New York, Rockefeller University Press, 1967. A collection of detailed symposium articles dealing with the relationship between brain mechanisms, endocrine systems, autonomic activity, infantile stimulation, and emotion.

James, W., and Lange, C. G. *The Emotions.* Baltimore, Williams & Wilkins, 1922. A collection of three works by these early pioneers: one defining emotion, the other two setting forth the theory associated with James and Lange.

Mandler, G. "Emotion," in *New Directions in Psychology,* 1. New York, Holt, Rinehart & Winston, 1962, pp. 267–343. An excellent review article that covers much the same areas as does this chapter, but in greater detail.

Murray, E. J. *Motivation and Emotion.* Englewood Cliffs, N. J., Prentice-Hall, 1964. A good, short introductory survey of emotion and motivation and the relation between them.

Schachter, S., and Singer, J. E. "Cognitive, Social and Physiological Determinants of Emotional State," *Psychological Review,* 69 (1962), pp. 379–399. The theory and the experiments that are at the core of the research mentioned in the final section of the last chapter.

How can you define a drive without using a circular definition? For example, define thirst without saying, "Thirst is the desire or tendency to get water," or, "Animals drink water because they are thirsty." These definitions are equivalent to saying that animals drink water because they are thirsty, which is the desire or tendency to get water.

How can you know if you are as thirsty as someone else? Could you measure thirst indirectly—for example, by the amount of work a person is willing to do for water? Would indirect measures be comparable between people?

18 Elementary Concepts of Motivation

HOW BEST TO QUENCH THIRST

When the salinity level of your cells is increased, you become thirsty. Some time must elapse after drinking before the homeostatic level is restored.

Make yourself thirsty. (How will you define how thirsty you are?) Soak your tongue in water (do not swallow) for ten seconds, then dry your tongue with a paper towel. Rate how thirsty you are (5 is very, and 1 is not); repeat soaking for twenty seconds, dry, and rate; repeat for thirty seconds, dry and rate. Does wetting the tongue reduce thirst?

Next, *squirt* one ounce of water down your throat (avoid your tongue). Rate your thirst. Repeat this twice. Does putting water down your throat reduce thirst? Then swallow normally one ounce, another ounce, and another of water, each time rating how thirsty you are.

Wait until you are thirsty again and time how long it takes, drinking as fast as possible, until you are no longer thirsty. How many seconds was it?

You are now in a position to discuss the factors involved in thirst. How is thirst turned off? What is necessary to turn it off? (What must be wetted?) How fast can it be turned off? Does this response indicate whether the action is neural or chemical?

Is hot water more thirst-quenching than cold water? How did you decide? How did you define thirst?

Eat normally, but don't drink anything. Do you notice a change in how hungry you feel? Does thirst interact with hunger?

FOOD FOR THE EMOTIONS

Pavlov found that animals will eat to reduce their fears. Does this provide an insight into why overweight people become that way? What are some implied negative psychological effects of dieting?

Eliminate salt or sweets from your diet for a few days. Do you get a salt or sweet craving? If so, how much of your craving is psychological? Are heavy people more stimulated than thin people by the visual aspects of food? Put some blue food coloring in milk and drink it. Rate how you liked it.

5	4	3	2	1
bothered me a lot				didn't bother me at all

Figure out what percent overweight you are by dividing pounds overweight by desired weight. (Underweight people will be minus pounds overweight.) If possible, pool class data for this experiment. Determine the correlation for the class between the scale value for blue milk and percent overweight. Does a relationship exist indicating that overweight people were bothered by the coloring more than were thin persons? What are the problems with this experiment as a test of the weight stimulus-effect theory?

DEALING WITH FEAR

Certain stimuli seem innately to trigger fear in animals. Are there any stimuli that innately trigger fear in humans? If so, how do we deal with these stimuli? For example, consider the purpose of a morgue.

NOTHING FAILS LIKE FAILURE

If a student drops a course because he is afraid to take an exam, why is this action likely to cause him to continue to drop out of his classes? What is the cure for his problem? (Hint: Escape behavior is usually very strong, because the person escaping is reinforced as long as he avoids the expected punishment.)

BASIC VERSUS LEARNED DRIVES

A long-standing question in psychology has asked which drives are basic; that is, not learned. The drives to sustain life are certainly basic, but sex is not necessary to life. The drives of fear and aggression are often thought to be basic.

Of greatest interest are the drives of curiosity and exploratory behavior. Monkeys and other animals will work to get a peek at a train or will sit for hours working puzzles. How could you test whether or not curiosity and exploratory drives are basic? Do you feel this is an important question?

SUGGESTED READINGS

Cofer, C. N., and Appley, M. H. *Motivation: Theory and Research.* New York, Wiley, 1964. This book gives a particularly thorough account of the historical antecedents to current research in hunger and thirst and their physiological correlates.

Deutsch, J. A., and Deutsch, D. *Physiological Psychology.* Homewood, Ill., Dorsey 1966. Provides an excellent overview of basic motivational states.

Gross, C. G., and Zeigler, H. P. (Ed.). *Readings in Physiological Psychology: Motivation.* New York, Harper & Row, 1969. An excellent book of readings.

Jones, M. R. (Ed.). *Nebraska Symposium on Motivation.* Lincoln, University of Nebraska Press. The Nebraska Symposia on Motivation, available in paperback, provide an annual treatment of current topics in motivation by experts currently working in the field.

Moyer, J. E. *The Physiology of Hostility.* Chicago, Markham, 1971. An excellent treatment of physiological and behavioral work in the general area of aggressive behavior.

Thompson, T., and Schuster, C. R. *Behavioral Pharmacology.* Englewood Cliffs, N. J., Prentice-Hall, 1968. An excellent overview of the effects of drugs upon behavior.

It is often difficult to differentiate emotion from motivation. A motive, especially when strong, can certainly involve feeling. And a strong emotion, such as anger, is powerfully motivating.

Can these terms be pinned down, or are they (as the behaviorists argue) useless concepts? Do you think the terms are useful?

Can we define all motives and emotions operationally; that is, by the operations leading to them? For example, anger results when goal behavior is blocked, and hunger is defined by the number of hours without food. If your have difficulty defining a term, is it useful? Should we use terms we cannot define?

19
Human
Motivation

SUBCONSCIOUS MOTIVATION REVEALED BY LAUGHTER

Laughter often releases tension and as such it often reveals hidden motivations. Says Jacob Levine in the February 1956 *Scientific American:*

> *Freud's theory, simply stated, says that humor gives pleasure by permitting the momentary gratification of some hidden and forbidden wish and at the same time reducing the anxiety that normally inhibits the fulfillment of the wish. By making light of the forbidden impulse, treating it as trivial or universal, a joke or cartoon releases inner tension. The sudden release of tension comes as a pleasant surprise, while the unconscious source of the individual's tension is so disguised in the joke that it is usually not disturbing.*

> *Sex and aggression are the main themes of humor because they are the primary sources of most human conflicts and tensions. It follows that a basic element in all humor is anxiety. The anxiety arises from inner conflicts over the inhibition of strong drives or impulses. A joke seems funny only if it arouses anxiety and at the same time relieves it. From this theory we can derive a hypothesis that there are three types of reaction to a joke or humorous happening. If it evokes no anxiety at all in an individual, either because he has no conflict over the subject or because his conflict is too deeply repressed, he will be indifferent to the joke. If the situation calls forth anxiety and immediately dispels it, the individual will find it funny. But if it arouses anxiety without dissipating it, he will react to the ostensibly humorous situation with disgust, shame, embarrassment, or horror. . .*

> *[T]he "mirth response test" we have employed has proved to be a useful instrument for probing personality and bringing out emotional problems. The test has been standardized as a set of 20 cartoons, and reactions to them are rated on a scale which we call the "mirth spectrum." The scale ranges from a negative grimace to a belly-laugh, with gradations in between, including no response, a half-smile, a smile, and so on. As the subject looks at each cartoon, the examiner notes his immediate reaction. Then the subject is asked to sort the cartoons into those he likes, dislikes, and views with indifference. Later he is interviewed on his understanding of each cartoon and the associations it evokes in his mind. His responses are then studied in relation to what is known about his background and personality.*

It is no easy matter to predict what cartoons will seem funny to a given person. But psychiatrists have found that they can predict pretty reliably which cartoons will disturb their patients. Undisguised sex. . ., gruesome aggression . . ., extreme prankishness and irreverence toward accepted authority (such as the police) are most often disturbing. However, persons whose sexual problems are close to the surface of awareness are apt to laugh boisterously—too readily and too loudly—at jokes about sex.

Choose one or two subjects and show them the jokes, both in written and cartoon form, that are reproduced on the following pages. They can be torn from the manual and separated, so that you can show them one at a time. They have varying themes that can be expected to evoke different responses in your subjects.

Were the cartoons that evoked a strong response of a consistent type for each subject? What would Levine say about each person's personality and hidden motives and emotions?

ACHIEVEMENT MOTIVATION IN AMERICANS

Is achievement motivation in America changing? Are women becoming more achievement-oriented, men less? What about minority and majority groups?

AN INDIRECT TEST OF MOTIVATION

Use the story completion task below to assess the motives of one or two subjects. Ask your subject to complete the following story with a short paragraph:

After the first term of class Anne/John finds herself/himself at the head of her/his medical school class.

(If your subject is female, use Anne; if male, use John.)

Examine the story. Does it tell you anything about the author's motives? In particular, does it reveal any of the motives below?

achievement	status
aggression	power
curiosity	love

SUGGESTED READINGS

Atkinson, J. W. (Ed.). *Motives in Fantasy, Action, and Society.* Princeton, N. J., Van Nostrand, 1958. An important book that pulls together the work done by many investigators on the various methods used to assess and study individual differences in various motivational dispositions, such as achievement, affiliation, and power. Scoring manuals and self-teaching materials are also included.

McClelland, D. *The Achieving Society.* Princeton, N. J., Van Nostrand, 1961. This book addresses the question of the social origins and consequences for society of achievement motivation.

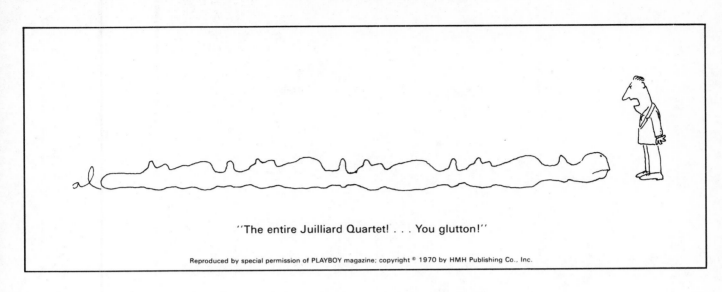

"The entire Juilliard Quartet! . . . You glutton!"

Two Village hippies: *"Look, baby, when we talk, do we always have to talk sex. Sex! Sex! Sex! Why can't we talk politics once in a while?"*

"O.K. Ah, how often do you think the leader of the opposition has intercourse?

*An old man was asked, "To what do you attribute your old age?" and he replied, "To the fact that I was born a long time ago." ***

Newsman: "Mr. Johnson, is it true that you were born in a log cabin?" LBJ: "No, you're thinking of Lincoln, he was born in a log cabin. I was born in a manger."

*From *When It's Laughter You're After,* by Stewart Harral. Copyright 1962 by the University of Oklahoma Press.

"I certainly don't see what you have to be grumpy about."

"Oh, *here* you are, Gloria! I said we'd meet you under the big *clock*!"

"For heaven's sake, can't you do anything right?"

Pablo Picasso relates the story of an American GI who met him in Paris and told Picasso that he didn't like modern paintings because they weren't realistic. The artist made no immediate reply. A few minutes later the soldier showed him a snapshot of his girl friend. "My word," exclaimed Picasso," is she really as small as all that?

Seems that Churchill, wobbly from a bout with brandy, was leaning for support against a marble pillar in a palatial mansion where he had been a dinner guest. A haughty, middle-aged dowager walked up to the careening statesman. "Mr. Churchill, you are drunk," she muttered contemptuously. "Yes, you are right," agreed Mr. Churchill. "But you, madame, are ugly. And in the morning I shall be sober."

Jack Paar once observed, "I grew up to be the kind of kid my mother didn't want me to play with."

Escher Foundation, Haags Gemeentemuseum, The Hague

UNIT VII
Personality

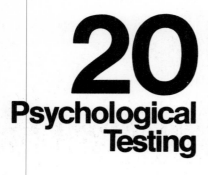

20
Psychological Testing

Measurement is the assignment of numbers to observed phenomena. Psychologists face many problems in trying to measure behaviors and feelings. For example, how might the following factors be measured?

the number of people in a room
height
the proportion of votes a candidate will receive
hunger
love
liberty

What makes each phenomenon difficult or easy to measure? What can you predict from this exercise regarding the difficulties of measuring personality and intelligence?

INTELLIGENCE—ONE FACTOR OR MANY?

There is probably no other single topic in psychology that has captured as much interest, had as much application, and led to as much controversy as the concept of intelligence. Psychologists are divided into three main camps regarding intelligence. Some believe there is, in fact, a general ability called intelligence; others, that intelligence is actually composed of many subintelligences, or *abilities*; and still others, that no universal concept of intelligence is possible—that intelligence is merely a score on a particular test. This last view receives increasing attention as cultural biases in intelligence testing are revealed.

The following are descriptions of four people who differ in intelligence.

Peter was always good with his hands and from a very early age could take apart almost anything mechanical and put it back together. An average student scholastically, Peter was content to spend most of his time in high school playing football and dating. He never achieved higher than a B in any class and had to repeat basic algebra; math was never his strongest subject.

Richard was a scholar in school. His superb memory brought him honors in almost all subjects except mathematics, in which he earned Bs and Cs. Geometry was especially difficult for Richard, because he finds it difficult to visualize geometric relationships. The thing that really frazzles him, however, is mechanical machinery. He has often described himself as "all thumbs," unable even to wire a plug.

Jane took top honors in the state for her mathematical prowess. She was capable of manipulating numbers from an early age. Mechanical things are perplexing to her but not unfathomable. Her most challenging subjects in school were those requiring a good memory; Jane's memory is average. Her friends feel she has a lot of common sense.

Darlene was an average student doing best in courses like art and journalism and only fair in abstract topics like math. Darlene is one of the best artists in the country; she is best known for her insight into color and spatial relationships. She is an accomplished potter as well. Her mechanical ability is mediocre.

(1) Rate each of these four people in general intellectual capacity:

	Genius						Retarded
Peter	7	6	5	4	3	2	1
Richard	7	6	5	4	3	2	1
Jane	7	6	5	4	3	2	1
Darlene	7	6	5	4	3	2	1

(2) People differ in the relative importance they attribute to specific traits in judging intelligence. When you rated the four people in (1), you may have implicitly assumed that all traits—from abstract reasoning to artistic ability—are equally important.

How important do you feel each of the twelve traits in Figure 20.1 is to intelligence? Assign each trait a weight of zero to 4, as specified below, and enter your trait ratings under "Importance weight" in Figure 20.1.

critical 4   very important 3   important 2

not very important 1   unimportant 0

Figure 20.1. Rating of four hypothetical persons on twelve traits relevant to intelligence.

FIGURE 20.1. INTELLIGENCE TESTING BY TRAIT						
Trait	Importance weight	Hi Lo X 7 6 5 4 3 2 1 =	Peter	Richard	Jane	Darlene
Ability to learn						
Abstract thinking[1]						
Creativity						
Verbal ability						
Memory						
Understanding commands						
Common sense						
Artistic ability						
Mechanical ability						
Spatial ability[2]						
Moral reasoning[3]						
Sensitivity[4]						
Sum (Intelligence Score) =						

[1] **Abstract thinking** is the ability to represent events with symbols and to manipulate these symbols. Logic and mathematics are two manifestations of this ability.

[2] **Spatial ability** is the capacity to "see" a figure in a new orientation and perspective (without turning the figure).

[3] **Moral reasoning** is the ability to make sound moral judgments.

[4] **Sensitivity** is the ability to perceive the feelings of other persons.

After you have given an importance weight to each trait, construct an overall intelligence scale as follows:

(a) Multiply each weight by 1 and *add.*
(b) Multiply each weight by 7 and *add.*

Your new scale ranges from a lowest possible score of the sum in (a) to a highest possible score of the sum in (b).

lowest possible score [   ]   highest possible score [   ]

Now rate each of the four persons described above on each of the individual trait scales in Figure 20.1. For each scale, multiply the rating you give each person by the weight you gave that scale, and enter the answer under the individual's name. When you have finished the ratings, add the twelve trait scores for each person and divide by 12. This total score is your rating of each person's intelligence.

Did you arrive at different ratings by the methods in (1) and (2)? Rank the four individuals according to the scores they received:

		Name	
Rank		*Overall intelligence (1)*	*Intelligence by trait (2)*
Most intelligent	1		
	2		
	3		
Least intelligent	4		

If scores and ranks are different for the two criteria, can you explain why? Which seems better—an overall rating or a trait scaling?

How did you arrive at your weights? To what extent do these weights reflect your own value judgments? Where did you get your opinions about what makes a person intelligent?

If intelligence is what an intelligence test measures (as some psychologists believe), how were you able to rate each person? How would you differentiate intelligence from achievement? Is IQ a series of separate, specific traits, or are these traits manifestations of some underlying factor? Whichever way you think intelligence is organized, did either of the measurents, (1) or (2), measure it to your satisfaction?

ACHIEVEMENT VERSUS ABILITY TESTS

It is no simple matter distinguishing between tests that measure ability and those that tap achievement. Scholastic grades seem clearly to measure achievement. Or do they? Do all courses require the same degree of achievement capacity? Of ability?

Intelligence tests are supposed to measure ability. But are they without achievement factors when the largest part of most intelligence tests is vocabulary?

CULTURAL BIASES IN TESTING

Take the two intelligence tests on pages 151-156. What kind of intelligence is each test measuring? (Refer to the traits listed in Figure 20.1.) To what extent is each an achievement test?

SOCIAL IMPLICATIONS OF INTELLIGENCE TESTING

Robert Rosenthal and Lenore Jacobson discovered that if teachers are (falsely) told a child's IQ is low, it actually drops over a one-year period. (Rosenthal and Jacobson described their findings in the 1966 issue of *Psychological Reports.*) Is it unwise, then, to tell teachers the IQ scores of their pupils? What good uses might be made of this knowledge?

Suppose we could grow children artificially and could select for certain types of intelligence and other abilities. What type of selection procedure would you prefer? On what principle would it be based—moral criteria, occupational quota, or what?

SUGGESTED READINGS

Allison, J., *et al.* (Eds.). *The Interpretation of Psychological Tests.* New york, Harper & Row, 1968. Presents a series of papers that together supply a good overview of psychological testing.

American Psychological Association. *Standards for Educational and Psychological Tests and Manuals.* Washington, D.C., American Psychological Association, 1966. Contains a thorough description of standards for psychological tests.

Buros, O. (Ed.). *Personality Tests and Reviews.* Highland Park, N.J., Gryphon Press, 1970. Contains descriptions and critical reviews of all existing personality tests. A source book for anyone who is searching for almost any type of personality test.

McReynolds, P. *Advances in Psychological Assessment.* Palo Alto, Calif., Science & Behavior Books, 1968. Contains a survey of recent advances in the measurement of personality and intelligence.

Meehl, P. E. *Clinical Versus Statistical Prediction: A Theoretical Analysis and Review of the Evidence.* Minneapolis, University of Minnesota Press, 1954. Can individual clinicians predict behavior on the basis of their intuition better then experimentalists on the basis of statistical evidence? Meehl supplies a thorough discussion of the evidence for both sides of the argument.

Schachtel, E. *Experiential Foundations of Rorschach's Test.* New York, Basic Books, 1966. Attempts to supply a theoretical foundation for the interpretation of the Rorschach ink-blot test. Schachtel's position is based on a theory of perception. Even if, as some have argued, his theory is faulty, the book presents a good introduction to the interpretation of the Rorschach Test.

Wechsler, D. *The Measurement and Appraisal of Adult Intelligence.* Baltimore, Williams & Wilkins, 1958. A classic discussion of intelligence and intelligence testing.

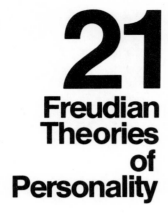

21
Freudian Theories of Personality

Freud's observations and theories had a major impact on our understanding of ourselves. Because of Freud, man began to recognize his unconscious motives and defenses.

UTOPIA AFTER FREUD

Plan a utopian society that would take into consideration the following:

Freud said pleasure is the basic need of the id. How would this need be fulfilled? (Don't foreget, people have to eat and keep warm.)

How would the ego be developed and satisfied? Would ego needs differ at the anal, oral, phallic, and genital stages of development?

How would the Oedipal problem be handled?

What rules would govern the superego?

How would the death instinct be handled?

What instinctual needs would be channeled off through displacements, and how?

Would anxiety be eliminated? Would all defense mechanisms be eliminated?

Would scientific research and higher education be continued?

Evaluate the society you have created. Would you be happy living in it?

LOVE

Where in Freud's paradigm is the concept of love? If what the world needs now is love, how could we get it, according to Freud?

AGGRESSION

Are we destined to be aggressive and destructive, according to Freud? What mechanisms could we use to direct our aggressive tendencies?

WHO WAS FREUD DESCRIBING, ANYWAY?

Freud's theory was based largely on observations during therapy with Victorian Viennese women. Do you think Freud would have formulated the same theory today? For example, are sexual needs still the main focus of our neurotic tendencies? Is aggression still as strong?

SUGGESTED READINGS

Hall, Calvin S., and Lindzey, Gardner. *Theories of Personality*. 2nd ed. New York, Wiley, 1970. The classic secondary source on theories of personality. It begins with a discussion of the nature of personality theory and outlines the theories of Freud, Jung, Adler, Fromm, Horney, Sullivan, Murray, Lewin, Allport, Goldstein, Angyal, Maslow, Lecky, Sheldon, Cattell, Skinner, Rogers, and several existential psychologists. Finally, it compares and contrasts theories across a number of dimensions and issues.

Levy, Leon H. *Conceptions of Personality*. New York, Random House, 1970. Levy's text on personality examines issues in personality theory rather than outlining theories of personality. It integrates a number of contemporary lines of research.

Maddi, Salvatore R. *Personality Theories, a Comparative Analysis*. Homewood, Ill., The Dorsey Press, 1968. A recent text on personality theory, it classifies personality theorists according to whether their basic assumption relates to *conflict* (Freud, Murray, Sullivan, Rank, Angyal, and Bakan), *fulfillment* (Rogers, Maslow, Adler, White, Allport, and Fromm) or *consistency* (Kelly, McClelland, Fiske, and Maddi), then goes on to examine what they have to say about the core and periphery of personality. It presents research on each position and draws conclusions about their strengths and weaknesses.

Maddi, Salvatore R. *Perspectives and Personalities: A Comparative Approach*. Boston, Little, Brown, 1971. A book of readings by or about each major theorist discussed in the Maddi text, cited above.

22
Other Theories of Personality

Why have other theories of personality developed since Freud's time? Many psychologists have thought Freudian theory inadequate to account for such factors as investigation behavior, competitiveness, and the interplay between man and his changing social environment.

THE DRIVING FORCE OF LIFE

One of the most important facets in all personality theories concerns the basic driving force behind human activities. Freud and Erikson posited the hedonistic principle that man's basic motivation is to achieve pleasure and avoid pain. White and Adler believed that man is impelled to explore his world, becoming competent in his society and overcoming feelings of inferiority. Jung argued man is driven by the desire to become a well-integrated individual. Fromm believes that man strives to achieve unity with nature.

Discuss the motivation behind each of the following activities. Whose theory best explains each?

> going camping
> listening to the sea
> becoming president
> helping a stranded motorist
> killing an animal for pleasure
> solving a picture puzzle
> going to school
> meditating
> playing cards
> committing rape
> (Don't read any further!)
> the reason you kept reading

Did one theory explain all these activities? Or is it possible the driving force behind life is more complicated than any one theory allows?

Jung believed we are unconsciously linked to our ancestral past. Can you think of any evidence for or against the "collective unconscious tendencies" Jung described? What does this concept imply is the basis of human happiness?

Why do you think children play? Would a Freudian explanation of play behavior differ from Adler's or White's?

UNDERSTANDING YOUR PERSONALITY

Indicate whether you think the following statements are true or false about you.

	True	False
(1) You have a great need for other people to like and admire you.	——	——
(2) You have a tendency to be critical of yourself.	——	——
(3) You have a great deal of unused capacity which you have not turned to your advantage.	——	——
(4) While you have some personality weaknesses, you are generally able to compensate for them.	——	——
(5) Your sexual adjustment has presented problems for you.	——	——
(6) Disciplined and self-controlled outside, you tend to be worrisome and insecure inside.	——	——
(7) At times you have serious doubts as to whether you have made the right decision or done the right thing.	——	——
(8) You prefer a certain amount of change and variety and become dissatisfied when hemmed in by restrictions and limitations.	——	——
(9) You pride yourself as an independent thinker and do not accept others' statements without satisfactory proof.	——	——
(10) You have found it unwise to be too frank in revealing yourself to others.	——	——
(11) At times you are extroverted, affable, sociable, while at other times you are introverted, wary, reserved.	——	——
(12) Some of your aspirations tend to be pretty unrealistic.	——	——
(13) Security is one of your major goals in life.	——	——

How effectively do you think these statements reveal the basic characteristics of your personality? The "test" was constructed by B. R. Forer, but not in the ordinary fashion. Forer wanted to demonstrate the ease with which people accept a diagnostic technique as credible, so he compiled the above thirteen statements largely from a newsstand astrology book. He gave identical copies of the statements to all the students in an introductory psychology class—as described in W. Leslie Barnette's book, *Readings in Psychological Tests and Measurements* (Chicago: Dorsey Press, 1964). Forer told his students that each had received a personalized sketch summarizing his responses to a personality test taken previously. Despite the vagueness of the statements, virtually all Forer's students indicated the statements accurately assessed their personalities.

Ask two or three others to respond to the statements. If other people are suspiciously unanimous in their agreement with the statements, it is because, although Forer's test may have *face validity*, it does not have what psychologists call *predictive validity*. The statements are so general in their applicability that they equally describe almost anyone.

SUGGESTED READINGS

Hall, Calvin S., and Lindzey, Gardner. *Theories of Personality*. 2nd ed. New York, Wiley, 1970. The classic secondary source on theories of personality. It begins with a discussion of the nature of personality theory and outlines the theories of Freud, Jung, Adler, Fromm, Horney, Sullivan, Murray, Lewin, Allport, Goldstein, Angyal, Maslow, Lecky, Sheldon, Cattell, Skinner, Rogers, and several existential psychologists. Finally, it compares and contrasts theories across a number of dimensions and issues.

Levy, Leon H. *Conceptions of Personality*. New York, Random House, 1970. Levy's text on personality examines issues in personality theory rather than outlining theories of personality. It integrates a number of contemporary lines of research.

Maddi, Salvatore R. *Personality Theories, a Comparative Analysis*. Homewood, Ill., The Dorsey Press, 1968. A recent text on personality theory, it classifies personality theorists according to whether their basic assumption relates to *conflict* (Freud, Murray, Sullivan, Rank, Angyal, and Bakan), *fulfillment* (Rogers, Maslow, Adler, White, Allport, and Fromm), or *consistency* (Kelly, McClelland, Fiske, and Maddi), then goes on to examine what they have to say about the core and periphery of personality. It presents research on each position and draws conclusions about their strengths and weaknesses.

Maddi, Salvatore R. *Perspectives and Personalities: A Comparative Approach*. Boston, Little, Brown, 1971. A book of readings by or about each major theorist discussed in the Maddi text, cited above.

Rate yourself along the following dimensions. Ask a friend and, if possible, also a stranger and a relative, to rate you along the same dimensions.

detached	1	2	3	4	5	6	7	participating
emotional	1	2	3	4	5	6	7	calm
mild	1	2	3	4	5	6	7	aggressive
serious	1	2	3	4	5	6	7	carefree
rule-free	1	2	3	4	5	6	7	rule-bound
introverted	1	2	3	4	5	6	7	extroverted
independent	1	2	3	4	5	6	7	dependent
trusting	1	2	3	4	5	6	7	distrusting
self-confident	1	2	3	4	5	6	7	self-doubting
conservative	1	2	3	4	5	6	7	liberal

How well do others' estimations of you compare with your own? If they differ much, is it because your self-concept and behavior differ? Do you play different roles for different people? What roles do you play?

IMPRESSION CUES

What is your impression of each person indicated on page 122?

	Impression				
Person	Highly favorable				Highly unfavorable
1	5	4	3	2	1
2	5	4	3	2	1
3	5	4	3	2	1
4	5	4	3	2	1
5	5	4	3	2	1
6	5	4	3	2	1

How important were the following factors in molding your impressions of these people?

   nonlinguistic aspects of speech (for example, emotion)
   proximity
   posture
   gestures
   facial expression
   eye contact

Did these features differ in importance, depending upon the sex of the person?

If possible, pool ratings in class and compare your six ratings with the class average for each of the six persons.

Person	Your rating	Class average
1		
2		
3		
4		
5		
6		

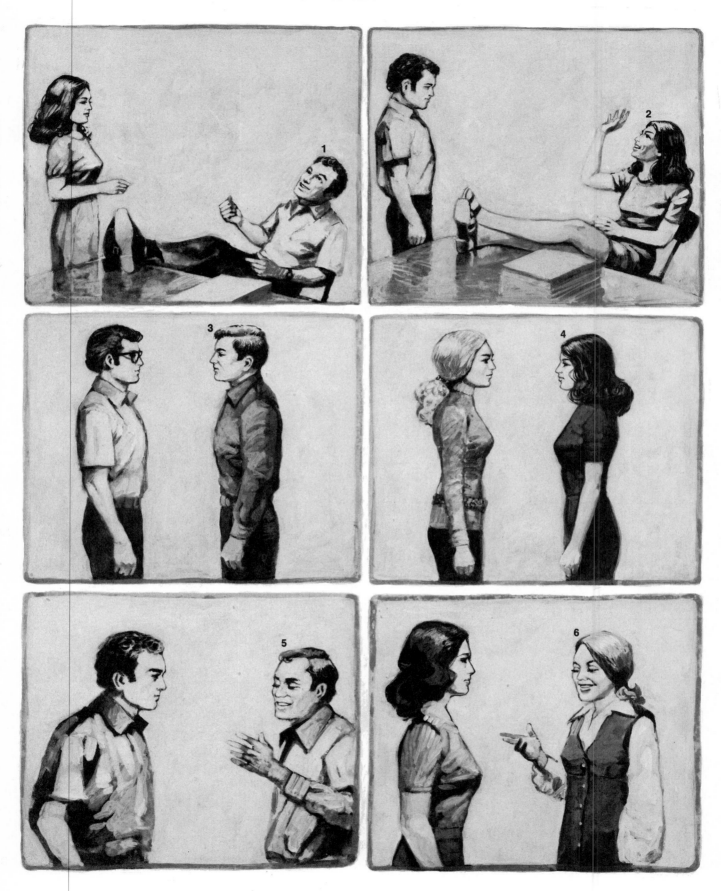

If your ratings are not representative of the class as a whole, could it be you see people differently than most of your classmates?

EFFECTS OF COMBINING TRAITS

Do traits add, average, or interact in some complex way? Find out by rating each trait separately below and then in the combinations specified. If possible, have several people try this.

Trait		Desirable			Undesirable	
Introverted	(A)	1	2	3	4	5
Aggressive	(B)	1	2	3	4	5
Loud	(C)	1	2	3	4	5
Bubbly	(D)	1	2	3	4	5
Well-mannered	(E)	1	2	3	4	5
A+B+C		1	2	3	4	5
A+C+D		1	2	3	4	5
A+D+E		1	2	3	4	5
B+C+D		1	2	3	4	5
B+C+E		1	2	3	4	5
C+D+E		1	2	3	4	5

Did the traits add, average, or do something else? What happened when conflicting traits were combined?

SUGGESTED READINGS

Fast, Julius. *Body Language.* New York, M. Evans & Co., 1970. An adequate first introduction to nonverbal communication—as long as the author's "conclusions" are translated to "possibilities."

Goffman, Erving. *The Presentation of Self in Everyday Life.* Garden City, N. Y., Doubleday, 1959. A classic in the study of how impressions are made. Goffman presents a creative and original description of everyday social interactions, with the theme, "Man Is an Actor." The book sacrifices theoretical perspective for description.

Goffman, Erving. *Stigma: Notes on the Management of Spoiled Identity.* Englewood Cliffs, N. J., Prentice-Hall, 1963. An analysis of people with something to hide; by extension, therefore, an examination of the role of others in the formation and maintenance of identity.

Hastorf, A. H., Schneider, D. J., and Polefka, J. *Person Perception.* Reading, Mass., Addison-Wesley, 1970. An excellent introduction to research on impression formation. Attribution theory and general issues in the study of the way people perceive other people.

Tagiuri, Renato, and Petrullo, Luigi (Eds.). *Person Perception and Interpersonal Behavior.* Stanford, Calif., Stanford University Press, 1958. A book of readings that is the outcome of the Harvard–Office of Naval Research Symposium on Person Perception, held at Harvard University in 1957. The twenty-three articles range from excerpts of the original thought of Fritz Heider to theoretical contributions of Edward Jones and John Thibaut and the methodological questions of Lee Cronbach. A classic in the field.

UNIT VIII
Social Psychology

24
The Individual and His Groups

See how long it takes two people (or more) working together and different people working separately to come up with solutions to the following problems.

Have two people play checkers. Have the loser of this match team up with a third person against the winner. Does this change affect the outcome?

Have two people take the test of creativity on page 58 together, and then ask two different people to take the same test individually. Which strategy is most successful? Might individual problem-solving be better suited to some types of tasks, teamwork to others?

It would be valuable to pool class data. Where are two heads better than one? Worse? For what real-life situations would you recommend think tanks?

Move all the rings from (c) to (a) without putting a larger on a smaller ring.

WHO ARE YOU?

Answer the question "Who am I?" in ten words or phrases. What does this exercise tell you about yourself?

UNDERSTANDING YOUR GROUP TIES

How important to you are each of the groups below?

	Very important				Not important
School	1	2	3	4	5
Religious	1	2	3	4	5
Work	1	2	3	4	5
Racial	1	2	3	4	5
Ethnic	1	2	3	4	5
National	1	2	3	4	5
Political	1	2	3	4	5
Family (parents or spouse and children	1	2	3	4	5
Social (e.g., fraternity)	1	2	3	4	5
Special interest group	1	2	3	4	5

How strongly would you feel about doing each of the following things? Rate as 5 if you would very much not want to do it; rate as 1 if the change would make no difference to you.

	Very undesirable				Not important
Leave school	1	2	3	4	5
Give up your religion	1	2	3	4	5
Transfer to a different job	1	2	3	4	5
Change your race	1	2	3	4	5
Change your ethnic background	1	2	3	4	5
Change your citizenship	1	2	3	4	5
Change your political affiliations	1	2	3	4	5
Change your parents or spouse and children	1	2	3	4	5
Quit your social group	1	2	3	4	5
Quit your special interest group	1	2	3	4	5

Correlate your ratings on these two scales, pairing same-numbered items. If the correlation is low, your intellectual concerns about your group ties may be different than your emotional feelings.

YOUR GROUPS

For each of three major groups you belong to:

   Is it a task or social group?

   What are the group goals?

   What are the symbols of cohesiveness used? Do they influence your feelings of belonging?

   What sacrifices, such as initiations or loss of liberties, does the group exact from members in building solidarity?

   What are the group's values? Would you retain them if not a member?

   What is the group's method of dealing with dissent? How would the group deal with an unpopular idea?

SUGGESTED READINGS

Brown, Roger. *Social Psychology.* New York, Free Press, 1965. This most readable of social-psychology textbooks is highly recommended. Of particular relevance to this chapter are Chapter 13 (Group Dynamics) and Chapter 14 (Collective Behavior and the Psychology of the Crowd).

Cartwright, Dorwin, and Zander, Alvin (Eds.). *Group Dynamics.* 3rd ed. New York, Harper & Row, 1968. An excellent collection of research reports on such topics as conformity, leadership, and power in groups; the editors have provided useful overviews of theory and research.

25
Patterns of Social Behavior: The Case of Sex Roles

Ask one male and one female to reverse sex roles and discuss the following contentions:

Women and men have equal sexual desires but women restrain them.

Men think love is attained through sex; women differ.

Women really want a playboy of the month but are embarrassed.

Men need liberation as much as women, because they inhibit emotions; must work harder and fight wars; do not share in the bearing and caring of children; cannot rely upon children as a life fulfillment, as can women, and must make a significant contribution outside the home; and have no life after work, whereas women's lives end with children.

Women don't mind being dominated as long as they are loved and cared for.

Women can never be as competent as men, or men as women, in which of the following?

> scientists
> child rearing
> tedious jobs
> jobs requiring constant vigilance (undisrupted by menstrual cycles)

SEX ROLES

Write a summary of the major misperceptions men and women have about each others' roles. What do you think is the desirable sex-role differentiation, if any?

How do the effects and content of sex roles change as a person grows older? Consider such stages as puberty, choosing a career, and childbearing.

Observe the diversity of sexual roles on the dimensions below for young children in any setting where children gather—nursery school, playground, and stores. Then observe adults in a social setting, such as a dining hall or party.

> dress (clothing, hair, jewelry)
> language (For example, do males use different language with groups of men than they do in mixed company?)
> gestures and posture (Do males and females sit or stand differently, interact at different distances, hold or throw things differently?)
> address (Do the forms with which people address each other vary across sex? Do other factors account for variations?)
> touch (Who touches whom, where, and when?)

Are people more likely to help a man or a woman in distress? Why?

Is total obliteration of all male-female discriminations and customs desirable?

SUGGESTED READINGS

Bem, S. L., and Bem, D. J. "We're all Nonconscious Sexists," *Psychology Today,* 4 (1970), pp. 22 ff. Two psychologists suggest that all Americans make sexist assumptions—often unwittingly—and they provide an interesting "test" for hidden sexist thinking.

Bird, C. *Born Female: The High Cost of Keeping Women Down.* New York, Pocket Books, 1969. A popular (profeminist) writer presents solid facts and figures on sex discrimination and the inferior status of American women.

How much is your life affected by persons with legitimate authority? Consider in your answer the military, police, teachers, doctors, scientists, clergymen, politicians.

26
Attitude Change and Social Influence

FINDING ATTITUDES WITH LOST LETTERS

You can find out how people feel about various interest groups by dropping stamped, unmailed letters in places where they are likely to be found—a technique developed by Stanley Milgram and described by him on pages 632-637 of *Readings in Psychology Today,* 2nd edition, 1972. We assume that people tend to mail letters of groups they like and destroy letters of groups they dislike.

Address five or ten letters to yourself placing the name of a group in favor of some attitude under the name of a fictitious sender. For example:

> M. Thuringer
> Students for Gun Controls
>
>
>
> (Your name)
> (Your address)

Address an equal number of letters to yourself indicating that M. Thuringer is with "Students Against Gun Controls." Put the same message in *all* letters. For example:

(Date)

Dear (your name):

We're having a noon meeting Friday at my place and look forward to your joining us for lunch.

Sincerely,
Max

Distribute the letters in conspicuous places, being careful not to favor one group of letters over another and to make each look accidentally lost. The more letters you distribute, the more accurate your findings will be. The results are easily determined by comparing the numbers of pro and con letters returned. Distribute a control group of letters indicating that M. Thuringer is with the Campus Chess Club or an equally noncontroversial group. You can measure almost any attitude with this technique—Whites for Black Power, Friends of Nixon, Fellowship Through

Drugs, or Parapsychology Research Group. If possible, perform this experiment before a local election. Tabulate your results and compare them to the outcome of the election.

FREEDOM OF SPEECH AND RESEARCH

How effective is the strategy of shouting down a very persuasive speaker who is advocating an action you consider morally wrong?

Does a scientist have the right to fool his subjects? Consider, for example, the effects on Stanley Milgram's subjects of believing they had harmed a fellow subject by obeying the orders of a stranger.

Does a scientist have a responsibility for what he discovers? Did nuclear physicists have an ethical duty to withhold the information needed to manufacture atomic bombs?

INOCULATION

Considering that beliefs grow stronger after the believer has heard counter-arguments, do you think it would be wise to describe in textbooks the domestic and foreign problems of the United States, past and present?

THE EFFECTS OF PACKAGING

Ask people to rank the desirability of the adjacent liqueur bottles. Pool class data to see if the shape of a bottle determines its desirability.

Obtain several brands of cigarettes, accomplished most economically if the class pools cigarettes. Blindfold a smoker. Can he identify his own brand? Alternatively, try a few brands of instant coffee on people who regularly drink instant. Can they tell the difference?

How would you go about testing whether today's generation is more or less conforming than previous ones? How will you define conforming? Has conformity always had a negative connotation? Will you consider in your test what people conform to?

SUGGESTED READINGS

Bem, Daryl J. *Beliefs, Attitudes, and Human Affairs.* Belmont, Calif., Brooks/Cole, 1970. An excellent and highly readable short text on attitudes and their social implications, including a good treatment of Bem's own self-perception theory.

Cohen, Arthur R. *Attitude Change and Social Influence.* New York, Basic Books, 1964. Although it is getting a bit dated, Cohen's book remains an excellent and thorough short text in this area.

Gergen, Kenneth J., and Marlowe, David (Eds.). *Personality and Social Behavior.* Reading, Mass., Addison-Wesley, 1970. Of relevance both to this chapter and to Chapter 27. A useful overview of theory and research linking individual personality to social processes like influence and attraction, plus a good collection of research reports on these topics.

Zimbardo, Philip, and Ebbesen, Ebbe. *Influencing Attitudes and Changing Behavior.* Reading, Mass., Addison-Wesley, 1969. Less systematic but more recent and readable than the Cohen text. Theory and research on social influence are applied to such varied contexts as psychological warfare, police confessions, and salesmanship.

Which of these bottles do you find most appealing? Why?

27
Interpersonal Attraction

Persons in solitary confinement often experience overwhelming anxiety. There appears to be something, for many people, about being alone that makes them anxious. In fact, one theory suggests that a basic reason for seeking companionship is the reduction of this kind of anxiety.

Isolate yourself for one to five hours. No other people should be nearby and no entertainment available, such as television or reading materials. Make notes of your thoughts and feelings as they unfold.

After your experience, write a paragraph describing how you felt and what you discovered about yourself. Were you bored with your own company? If you were, how did you overcome the boredom? Should people be able to be alone with themselves for short intervals and be comfortable? Do you ever look forward to being alone? What is the difference between being alone and loneliness? Have you ever felt lonely in the company of others?

THE DIMENSIONS OF ATTRACTION

Rate how much you would like to meet each of the people in the adjacent photograph.

very much ————————————————————— not at all
       100   50   0

How much would you like to be friends with each person?

very much ————————————————————— not at all
       100   50   0

Did personal appearance influence your ratings of people of your sex? For people of the opposite sex? You can learn how similar your standards of attraction are to those used by your classmates by pooling your results in class. Rate each of the acquaintances you know best on the following scale:

I like this person

very much ——————————————————— not at all   Score
       100   50   0   from
                                                               scale

Now rate each of these people on the following attributes:

physical attractiveness   Hi —————————————— Lo
                                   100   50   0

similar values (to your own) Hi —————————————— Lo
                                   100   50   0

similar attitudes   Hi —————————————— Lo
                                   100   50   0

similar knowledge   Hi —————————————— Lo
                                   100   50   0

similar interests   Hi —————————————— Lo
                                   100   50   0

How much would you like to meet each of
these people? To be friends with each person?
How attractive is each?

Correlate the likeability score for each acquaintance with his or her scores on each
of the other attributes (five correlations in all—review page xiii). How important is
attractiveness to you in making friends? Are other factors equally or more
important? Does the importance you place on physical attractiveness vary in
meeting people, making friends, dating, and marriage?

To learn what you find physically attractive about people, thumb through
several magazines and note what features you find attractive in pictures of people,
keeping track of your affinities on Chart 27.1, page 134.

THE DEFINITION OF LOVE

One of the most difficult emotions to define is love. Harry Stack Sullivan said that
"when the satisfaction and security of another person becomes as significant to one
as is one's own satisfaction, then the state of love exists." Do you agree with this
definition? Is there one type of love or many? If more than one, does Sullivan's
definition include all the forms love can take?

What do you find physically attractive about the same sex, the opposite sex?
To find out how your criteria compare with those used by classmates, pool your
results in class.

SUGGESTED READINGS

Berscheid, E., and Walster, E. H. *Interpersonal Attraction.* Reading, Mass., Addison-Wesley,
1969. A thorough and well-organized overview of theory and research in this area.
Heider, F. *The Psychology of Interpersonal Relations.* New York, Wiley, 1958. A classic
analysis of interpersonal behavior from the point of view of the individual actor. It presents
Heider's influential "balance theory" of interpersonal sentiments. The reading is sometimes
difficult, but it is well worth the effort.

		SAME SEX	OPPOSITE SEX
FACE	Eyes		
	Nose		
	Mouth		
	Skin		
	Hair		
	Ears		
BODY	Hands		
	Arm		
	Shoulders		
	Chest		
	Waist		
	Hips		
	Buttocks		
	Thighs		
	Legs		
	Ankles		
	Feet		
	Clothes		
	Arms		

Hunt, M. *The Natural History of Love.* New York, Knopf, 1959. A highly entertaining account of the history of love and courtship in the Western world, from the Golden Age of ancient Greece to modern times.

Jones, E. E. *Ingratiation: A Social-Psychological Analysis.* New York, Appleton-Century-Crofts, 1964. An excellent theoretical analysis and report of research on the tactics that people use to win approval from others.

Schachter, S. *The Psychology of Affiliation.* Stanford, Calif., Stanford University Press, 1969. A readable report of a classic series of experiments on the roots of human gregariousness.

Chart 27.1. Which of these features do you consider important in judging people attractive or unattractive?

28
Intergroup Behavior

The basic message of the Robbers Cave experiment is that competition causes hostility and cooperation leads to friendship. What implications does this message suggest about American society? What do you think about the following conclusions?

Students should not compete in school but should participate in cooperative projects and not receive grades.

The American business system should be converted from a competitive system to a communal or cooperative system.

Inequalities in private property represent a competitive attitude and should be abolished.

Should the concept of race be dropped entirely from the U.S. census? If not, what function is served by retaining it?

STEREOTYPES

Ask ten people to rate the type of person who smokes each of ten brands of cigarettes on the following traits:

young-old	thin-fat
masculine-feminine	cautious-striving
introvert-extrovert	high status-low status

ETHNOCENTRISM TEST

Compare the United States to other countries, rating the following achievements on a scale of five:

	America is best				America is worst
(1) ability to make products	5	4	3	2	1
(2) values governing daily life	5	4	3	2	1
(3) motivation for living	5	4	3	2	1
(4) moral standards	5	4	3	2	1
(5) generosity	5	4	3	2	1
(6) altruism	5	4	3	2	1
(7) scientific ideas	5	4	3	2	1
(8) cultural contributions	5	4	3	2	1
(9) equality of citizens	5	4	3	2	1
(10) racial tolerance	5	4	3	2	1
(11) religious tolerance	5	4	3	2	1
(12) opportunity for happiness	5	4	3	2	1
(13) cleanliness	5	4	3	2	1
(14) manners	5	4	3	2	1
(15) style of dress	5	4	3	2	1

	America is best				America is worst
(16) humility	5	4	3	2	1
(17) general satisfaction of citizens	5	4	3	2	1
(18) freedom to choose government	5	4	3	2	1
(19) ability to influence laws	5	4	3	2	1
(20) purity	5	4	3	2	1
(21) value of human life	5	4	3	2	1

After taking the test yourself, give it to three others, preferably people who differ from you in age, sex, or political attitudes. Average the scores for yourself and each of your subjects. For a stronger scale, tally scores for items 2, 3, 4, 5, 6, 12, 13, 14, 15, 16, 17, 20, and 21 as a separate scale. An average of three indicates no feeling that your country is inherently superior. An average greater than three indicates a preference for the United States, especially in response to the shorter scale. Less than three indicates an anti-American attitude, particularly on the shorter scale. What determines these attitudes? Did sex, age, or political party seem to matter? It is suggested that this data be pooled for the class, calculating separate averages for five-year age categories.

INTERRACIAL CONTACT AND ATTITUDES

Experience suggests that laws can, in fact, change the hearts of men. Enforced integration in several housing experiments have resulted in informal contact, awareness of intergroup similarities and shared goals, cooperation, and, finally, to more positive racial attitudes. What is your opinion about legally enforcing racial integration in housing, employment, and schools? Did the results, just cited, of enforced integration in housing experiments influence your attitudes?

Members of Third-World minorities in the United States have clearly had, and continue to have, more difficulty developing the necessary skills and motivation to do well at school and work. To compensate for their disadvantages, should minority members

face lower college admission standards?
satisfy lower graduation standards?
have preferential status on dormitory waiting lists?
meet lower hiring standards?
qualify for subsidies when renting or buying housing?

YOUR STEREOTYPE QUOTIENT

How do you characterize members of the race you do *not* belong to?

	Much more than my race		Same as my race	Much less than my race	
Lazy	5	4	3	2	1
Irresponsible	5	4	3	2	1
Intellectually inferior	5	4	3	2	1
Unclean	5	4	3	2	1
Angry	5	4	3	2	1
Unartistic	5	4	3	2	1
Insensitive	5	4	3	2	1
Physically weak	5	4	3	2	1
Impotent	5	4	3	2	1
Overly aggressive	5	4	3	2	1
Hostile	5	4	3	2	1
Animalistic	5	4	3	2	1
Uncultured	5	4	3	2	1
Cold	5	4	3	2	1
Fearful	5	4	3	2	1

Average your scores on these scales. A composite score greater than three indicates a prejudice toward your race. You are prejudiced against your own race if you score below three. Where did you get your racial attitudes?

SUGGESTED READINGS

Allport, G. *The Nature of Prejudice.* Garden City, N. Y., Anchor Books, 1958. A classic but still vital analysis of different approaches to the study of prejudice and of the basic psychological processes involved.

Deutsch, M., Katz, I., and Jensen, A. (Eds.). *Social Class, Race and Psychological Development.* New York, Holt, Rinehart and Winston, 1968. Fairly long articles by several noted psychologists on the ways in which race and social class affect intellectual development and a discussion of the psychological processes underlying these effects. Also includes articles on the scientific definition of race and on the education of the disadvantaged.

Grier, W. H., and Cobbs, P. M. *Black Rage.* New York, Bantam, 1969. Two black psychiatrists present their views of what it means psychologically to be black in America in a book that is liberally sprinkled with details of the life histories of their patients.

Kelman, H. C. (Ed.). *International Behavior: A Social-Psychological Analysis.* New York, Holt, Rinehart and Winston, 1965. New applications of the social-psychological concepts presented in this chapter—such as stereotypes and the effects of contact—are provided by this collection of articles on international relations.

Mack, R. (Ed.). *Race, Class and Power.* New York, American Book, 1968. A large assortment of short articles, both theoretical and empirical, on aspects of intergroup relations ranging from stereotypes in Brazil to the causes of race riots in America.

Marx, G. T. *Protest and Prejudice.* New York, Harper Torchbook, 1969. A survey of the attitudes of black Americans toward the civil rights movement and black militancy, and toward white Americans.

Pettigrew, T. *Profile of the Negro American.* New York, Van Nostrand Reinhold, 1964. A social psychologist discusses racial differences in health, intelligence and crime, and applies concepts such as social role and relative deprivation to American race relations.

Do you think encounter groups should be a regular part of everyone's education, perhaps a required subject? How useful would they be at work? In government? As a way of life?

Is it embarrassing for you to touch a member of the same sex? If so, why do you feel this way?

Stare at a friend's eyes for several minutes. How long were you able to sustain eye contact? Was it a disturbing experience? If possible, try this with several friends: What does the encounter tell you about each friendship?

29
Intensive Groups

INTERPERSONAL RELATIONSHIPS

The television program *All in the Family* portrays the interactions of a "typical" WASP family. Tally the number of interactions between each two members of the Bunker family. From your data, draw a sociogram of the interaction in this "family," the thickness of each interconnecting line indicating the frequency of that interaction. Try to place in the center whichever person is spoken to most frequently.

For example, your tally might look something like the following, excluding Mrs. Bunker for simplicity:

father speaks to daughter: 10
daughter to father: 50
son-in-law to father: 40
father to son-in-law: 5
son-in-law to daughter: 20
daughter to son-in-law: 10

From these figures, your sociogram should resemble the configuration below.

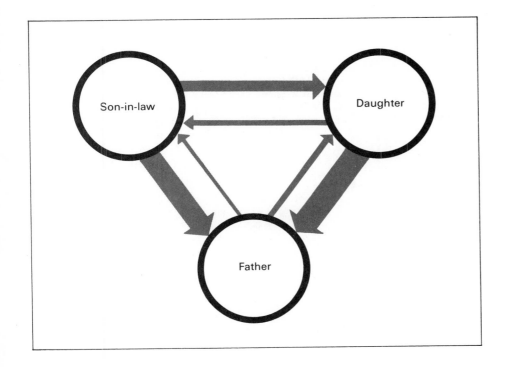

If it is easier for you, tally the Bunker family interactions in Table 29.1. (A tally in the upper-lefthand cell indicates the father talks to himself. You may want to exclude this type of cell from consideration.)

What does your sociogram tell you about the group's interactions? Who is the most popular person? Does communication divide by age, sex, or family status? Who talks to outsiders?

Alternatively, keep a similar tally of the intercommunications in any group to which you have access—roommates, athletic team, class, clique of friends, or family. Draw a sociogram of the interaction patterns.

Table 29.1. Tally the interactions of the Bunker family in the television series *All in the Family*.

	TO (ADDRESSED PERSON)						
FROM	Father	Mother	Daughter	Son-in-law	Outsider 1	Outsider 2	Outsider 3
Father							
Mother							
Daughter							
Son-in-law							
Outsider 1							
Outsider 2							
Outsider 3							

SUGGESTED READINGS

Bales, R. F. *Personality and Interpersonal Behavior.* New York, Holt, Rinehart and Winston, 1970. Probably the best theoretical and methodological system for understanding the interrelationships of members of the internal structure in small groups of all sorts.

Gibb, J. R. "Sensitivity Training as a Medium for Personal Growth and Improved Interpersonal Relationships," *Interpersonal Development,* 1 (1970), 6-31. A recent, comprehensive analysis and review of the research on the effects of experiences in intentional psychological groups.

Schein, E. H. *Process Consultation: Its Role in Organizational Development.* Reading, Mass., Addison-Wesley, 1969. A practical guide to understanding how the psychological (or form or process) requirements of any group can be recognized to make interaction more effective and to help the group reach its goals.

Slater, P. E. *Microcosm: Structural, Psychological, and Religious Evolution in Groups.* New York, Wiley, 1966. Slater emphasizes the deep symbolic meanings of group development, relating experiences in modern-day intentional psychological groups to religious myths and primitive societies.

Yalom, I., and Lieberman, M. "A Study of Encounter Group Casualties," *Archives of General Psychiatry,* 25 (1971), 16-30. An experimental comparison of many different styles of T-groups and some of their unfortunate consequences.

UNIT IX
Behavior Disorders and Therapy

30
Adjustment and Disorder

Two basic questions that have been debated hotly for many years by clinical psychologists concern the definition of abormality and diagnostic classifications. Psychoses are usually defined in terms of words that indicate a person is out of touch with reality, but deviant behavior is, simply, that not exhibited by most people.

In what sense is masturbation, which is universally practiced by almost all males and widely by females, considered deviant? If the majority do it, why is it deviant? Wouldn't a priest who chooses to remain celibate be deviant in this case, because he adopts an atypical sexual role?

Formulate a definition of mental illness. Is your definition free of social values, or are values a necessary part of the definition?

Would a person who lives in a tormented world of imaginary sounds and sights be called schizophrenic? What if great art, literature, or music were the outcome?

THE LANGUAGE OF SCHIZOPHRENIA

Do unconscious motives prevent the schizophrenic from communicating by language in the usual manner? Is the disorganization of his speech intentional? Is it a representation, in the form of a mirror image, of his thought processes themselves? Is it neither? According to Brendan Maher in *Readings in Psychology Today,* 2nd edition, 1972, pp. 549-553, schizophrenic utterances can be analyzed rationally. For example, consider the sentence at the bottom of this and the following page.

Where a punning word occurs at a vulnerable point, the sequence becomes disrupted and disintegrates into associative chaining until it terminates. The emotional significance of what the schizophrenic plans to say may have little or no bearing on when an intrusion occurs or what it seems to mean.

Compare the above sentence to the type of sentence structure in John Lennon's *In His Own Write* or *A Spaniard in the Works,* in James Joyce's *Ulysses,* in Bob Dylan's song "Hard Rain's A-gonna Fall," and in Dylan Thomas' poem "Ballad of the Long-Legged Bait." How relative are our notions of normality and abnormality?

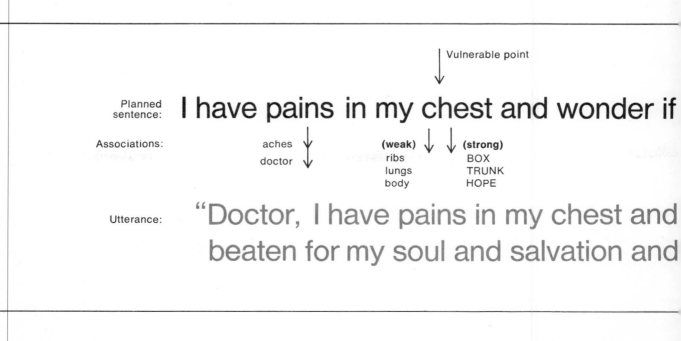

Vulnerable point

Planned sentence: I have pains in my chest and wonder if

Associations:
aches
doctor

(weak)
ribs
lungs
body

(strong)
BOX
TRUNK
HOPE

Utterance: "Doctor, I have pains in my chest and beaten for my soul and salvation and

THE MENTAL PATIENT AS A NONPERSON

The treatment of neurosis does not typically begin with classification of the patient as a certain type, such as a chronic worrier. The therapist works with each patient as an individual. What purpose do you think classification serves in psychoses? That is, why doesn't the therapist treat each psychotic case as unique?

SOCIETY AND DISORDER

How would you distinguish a sociopath from a person who consciously rebels against societal laws and norms he considers unreasonable?

Would you label as psychopathic a person who murders innocent people by dousing them with flammable liquid and setting them afire? What if he did it during wartime with napalm from an airplane? Why is the same behavior judged criminally insane in some circumstances and heroic in others?

How can voyeurism be considered abnormal behavior when *Playboy* sells so widely on the newsstands?

SUGGESTED READINGS

Kisker, G. W. *The Disorganized Personality*. New York, McGraw-Hill, 1964. The best elementary textbook on abnormal psychology. Well-written and well-illustrated, it contains a series of case histories to demonstrate types of disorder and presents an excellent discussion of the history of mental illness. Chapters follow the major categories in the diagnostic manual of the American Psychological Association.

Szasz, T. *The Myth of Mental Illness: Foundations of a Theory of Personal Conduct*. New York, Dell, 1961. A highly original, extremely stimulating discussion of mental illness. Szasz argues that what is commonly called mental illness really involves only problems in living.

White, R. W. *The Abnormal Personality*. New York, Ronald, 1964. A comprehensive, easy-to-read presentation of theories and research on abnormal behavior. Written by one of the pillars of classic personality theory, the book is pervaded by the force of Robert White's own personality. It contains an excellent presentation of psychoanalysis and learning theory.

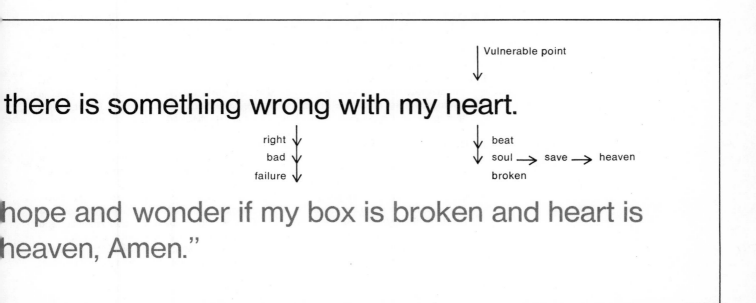

31
Bases
of Disorder

How would Freudian and social-learning theories differ in their treatment of the concept of repression? Would a Freudian be as apt to put a compulsive overweight eater on a diet as would a social-learning therapist? How do Freudian and social-learning theories differ in the meanings they attach to neurotic symptoms?

FROM BAD TO WORSE: SYMPTOM SUBSTITUTION

A social-learning theorist urges a patient to overcome his fear of injections by taking a biology course that requires the patient to take frequent blood samples from himself. The patient follows this advice and loses his fear of needles, but the cure intensifies his fear of knives. How would a Freudian explain this effect?

IT RUNS IN THE FAMILY

Some researchers have concluded, after studying twins separated from birth, that certain mental diseases are inherited. What factors would experimenters have to be careful of in drawing these conclusions? (Hint: Twins look alike, and people might react similarly to persons who look alike.)

THE ETHICS OF EXPERIMENTATION ON HUMANS

Suppose a researcher believes that the blood serum factor Xybotal when in imbalance causes a type of mental illness, which currently affects thousands of persons. There is only one way he can test his theory—by operating on subjects to cause a permanent Xybotal imbalance and consequent mental illness. He has a volunteer and you are the director of the clinic where the research would be conducted. Will you permit it? What are your reasons?

SUGGESTED READINGS

Cameron, N. *Personality Development and Psychopathology*. Boston, Houghton Mifflin, 1963. This work provides the reader with an understanding of how the psychoanalytically oriented clinician views psychological development and its relation to psychological disorders. It is a relatively complete presentation but can be easily understood by the unsophisticated reader.

Fenichel, O. *The Psychoanalytic Theory of Neurosis*. New York, Norton, 1945. This comprehensive and well-written presentation of the psychoanalytic theory of psychological disorder continues to be one of the standard reference books. When used as a text it is most appropriate at the graduate school level. However, its clear and precise presentation makes it useful for others who wish to thoroughly pursue a specific topic—for example, anxiety.

Kaplan, B. (Ed.). *The Inner World of Mental Illness*. New York, Harper & Row, 1964. This book contains a collection of descriptions of what it is like to have a psychological disorder. Each is written by the person who experienced the disorder. This volume is invaluable for the student who wants to understand what it is like to have a psychological disorder.

Maher, B. A. *Principles of Psychopathology: An Experimental Approach*. New York, McGraw-Hill, 1966. This unique volume reviews much of the research in the area of psychopathology. It represents an attempt to provide a basis for understanding and researching psychological disorders in terms of more general psychological processes. It is written for advanced undergraduate and graduate level students. However, any student wishing to thoroughly explore specific topics will find this volume to be a valuable source.

There are several forms of psychotherapy, including the following:

client-centered therapy
psychoanalytic-oriented psychotherapy
ego therapy
existential therapy
cognitive therapy
behavior therapy
gestalt therapy
encounter groups
psychoanalytic groups
family groups
marriage counseling

32 & 33
Psychotherapies

BUILDING A THERAPY

You are an eclectic therapist willing to draw on any of the therapeutic methods. For each of the patients described below, who have come to you for help, decide upon a course of therapy from those listed above. You may use more than one. Describe the reason for your decision.

John R. is a successful businessman who has risen rapidly to the top of the business world. He suddenly finds he has lost interest in his work as well as in the material gains his success has brought him. Although he is not deeply depressed, John finds a deepening sadness filling his days.

Mary S. has come to you because of a horrible dream that recurs at least once a week. Mary dreams that her mouth is covered with blood that she somehow knows is not her own. At this point in most of her dreams, Mary awakes with the physiological symptoms that usually accompany nightmares, such as vigorous sweating. With less frequency, she dreams that blood pours forth from her mouth, and she awakens from this nightmare in hysterics. Although her daily life is satisfactory to her, she is terrified to go to sleep and seeks your help.

Richard W. has a seemingly unfounded fear of airconditioning units, especially the watercooled type that features a large, rotating squirrel-cage blower assembly. He is often embarrassed when his friends notice how visibly shaken he appears whenever he passes by even a small window unit. He once walked past a large, open evaporative cooler and felt faint.

Robert M. sees himself as an undesirable person and finds his interpersonal relationships lacking. He has few friends and feels he is an abrasive person. He is very eager to change his personality to a more likable one but lacks an understanding of which of his behaviors are objectionable and what traits are desirable substitutions.

THE PSYCHIATRIC EXPERIENCE

Most articles and books about psychiatric treatment are written by doctors in the profession. But what is it like to be in a mental hospital from a patient's point of view? This question is explored in the following books, in which informed individuals discuss their psychiatric experiences.

Balt, John. *By Reason of Insanity*. New York, New American Library, 1966.

Freeman, Lucy. *Fight Against Fears*. New York, Crown, 1951.

Green, Hannah. *I Never Promised You a Rose Garden*. New York, Holt, Rinehart and Winston, 1964.

Kesey, Ken. *One Flew Over the Cuckoo's Nest*. New York, Viking, 1962.

Stefan, Gregory. *In Search of Sanity*. New Hyde Park, N. Y., University Books, 1965.

SUGGESTED READINGS

Arieti, S. (Ed.). *American Handbook of Psychiatry*. 3 vols. New York, Basic Books, 1959. Volume II of this series contains a discussion of the various schools of psychotherapy—for example, existential, group, psychodrama, psychoanalytic, and shock therapy. It also contains chapters that discuss mental hospitals and the general field of social work.

Bandura, A. *Principles of Behavior Modification*. New York, Holt, Rinehart and Winston, 1969. An extensive discussion of behavior therapy by one of the prime researchers in the field. It contains an especially good discussion of the effect of modeling.

Bergin, A. E., and Garfield, S. L. *Handbook of Psychotherapy and Behavior Change: an Empirical Analysis*. New York, Wiley, 1971. The most comprehensive collection of readings on psychotherapy. It contains sections on theory and methods of experimentation in psychotherapy; analysis of client-centered, psychoanalytic, eclectic, and related therapies; analysis of behavior therapies; and a series of papers that discusses therapeutic approaches in the home, family, school, group, organization, and community. Supplies the single best critical overview of the field.

Frank, J. *Persuasian and Healing: a Comparative Study of Psychotherapy*. Baltimore, The John Hopkins Press, 1961. An excellent discussion of the historical roots of psychotherapy and its cross-cultural counterparts. Analyzes psychotherapy in the context of religious healing and explores its relationship to shamanism. Examines various types of psychotherapy, experimental studies on psychotherapy, and the role of hospitals.

Goffman, E. *Asylum*. Garden City, N. Y., Doubleday, 1961. A highly original, sociological analysis of institutions that presents mental illness as an act played out to fulfill the expectations of institutional custodians.

Haley, J. *Strategies of Psychotherapy*. New York, Grune & Stratton, 1963. Stimulating discussion that argues that one primary goal of the psychotherapist is to help manipulate his patients. Patients' symptoms are analyzed as tactics in human relationships.

May, R., *et al.* (Eds.). *Existence*. New York, Clarion Books of Simon and Schuster, 1967. A series of papers by existential psychologists that captures the core and diversity of their positions.

Raush, H. C., and Raush, C. L. *The Halfway House Movement: A Search for Sanity*. New York, Appleton-Century-Crofts, 1968. The most complete discussion of the halfway house movement presently out. Contains an analysis of existing data on halfway houses and argues strongly for increasing their use.

Rogers, C. *Client-Centered Therapy*. Boston, Houghton Mifflin, 1951. A classic on client-centered therapy. Presents the complete position along with chapters on the applications of client-centered therapy to play therapy, group therapy, and student-centered therapy, and also includes a section on the training of client-centered therapists.

Schofield, W. *Psychotherapy: the Purchase of Friendship*. Englewood Cliffs, N. J., Spectrum Books of Prentice-Hall, 1964. Presents the argument that the primary need of patients is friendship. Suggests that the need for therapists should be filled in the community.

Wolman, B. (Ed.). *Handbook of Clinical Psychology*. New York, McGraw-Hill, 1965. Section 5 contains a series of papers on the methods of treating mental illness.

In *Brave New World* Aldous Huxley describes a world in which unpleasant emotions are nonexistent, because they are erased with drugs. The tonnage of tranquilizers, stimulants, and narcotics consumed in the United States seems to indicate we are well underway to achieving that blissful state. Or are we? Discuss the benefits and problems of a culture that relies so heavily on drug usage. Is drug usage a cure or a symptom?

34
Drugs and Drug Therapy

DOES PSYCHOLOGY SUGGEST THE ANSWER?

As a scientist of human behavior, you are called upon to apply your knowledge of psychology to solve the illicit drug problem in the United States. In planning a solution, consider what you know about learning, including conditioning; intelligence and problem solving; human motivation; and social psychology.

Back up your proposal with examples of solutions that have worked for similar problems as well as alternatives that have failed. Do you feel psychologists could solve problems of dangerous drugs and other social problems using your approach? If your answer is no, explain why. If your answer is yes, describe what role the psychologist would play. Do you feel he plays this role now?

SUGGESTED READINGS

Clark, W. G., and del Giudice, J. (Eds.). *Principles of Psychopharmacology*. New York, Academic Press, 1970. A general reference textbook.

Cooper, J. R., Bloom, F. E., and Roth, R. H. *The Biochemical Basis of Neuropharmacology*. New York, Oxford University Press, 1970. Review of the scientific data and theory underlying present-day neuropharmacology.

Dishotsky, N. J., *et al.* "LSD and Genetic Damage," *Science*, 172 (1971), 431–440. Reviewing the literature and reporting their own findings on the aspects of the toxicology of LSD.

Freedman, D. X. "The Use and Abuse of LSD," *Archives of General Psychiatry*, 18 (1968), 300–347. A thorough and complete review of LSD that is scholarly yet readable by a lay audience.

Goodman, L. S., and Gilman, A. *The Pharmacological Basis of Therapeutics*. 4th ed. New York, Macmillan, 1970. A general reference text book.

Greenblatt, M., *et al.* (Eds.). *Drug and Social Therapy in Chronic Schizophrenia*. Springfield, Ill., Charles C. Thomas, 1965. Interesting comparisons between the effects of drugs and psychosocial therapies in the treatment of chronic schizophrenia.

Grinspoon, L. *Marijuana Reconsidered*. Cambridge, Mass., Harvard University Press, 1970. A general but fairly thorough treatment of the subject, written mainly for the lay audience.

Jellinek, F. M. *The Disease Concept of Alcoholism*. New Haven, Conn., Hillhouse Press, 1960. A general review.

Klein, D. F., and Davis, J. M. *Diagnosis and Drug Treatment of Psychiatric Disorders*. Baltimore, Williams & Wilkins, 1969. A matter-of-fact presentation of the use of medicines in the treatment of mental illness.

Schildkraut, J. J., and Kety, S. S. "Biogenic Amines and Emotion," *Science*, 156 (1967), 21–30. A review of the catecholamine theory of affective illness.

Appendix

The Bell
"All-American"
Intelligence Test

1. The opposite of abhorrent is
   (a) remarkable (b) huge (c) appealing (d) soft (e) creative

2. Intricate is to simple as beautiful is to
   (a) several (b) ugly (c) misguided (d) lovely

3. If you make a purchase of a $20 item and the clerk adds a 4 percent sales tax, how much will you have to pay?
   (a) $24.00 (b) $21.00 (c) $20.80 (d) $18.95

4. Supply the next number in the following series.
   2   8   3   27   4   64   5

5. If a salesman gets a 10 percent commission on every radio he sells, how much will he have at the end of a day during which he has sold four radios worth $30 each and one radio worth $60?
   (a) $18.00 (b) $30.00 (c) $15.50 (d) $45.00

6. On a given map, one mile is represented by ⅛ inch. If the map shows a distance of 8½ inches between two cities, how long will the real distance be?
   (a) 68 miles (b) 160 miles (c) 8½ miles (d) 17 miles

7. Monday is to Wednesday as
   (a) month is to year (b) week is to month (c) February is to April
   (d) January is to February

8. The opposite of evanescing is
   (a) appearing (b) making poetry (c) praying (d) painting
   (e) eavesdropping

9. Benign means
   (a) holy (b) kind (c) exact (d) cruel

10. Supply the next number in the following series.
    8   6   16   14   32   30   64

11. The drawings in the first row form a series. In the second row, select the drawing that belongs where the question mark appears.

    (a)   (b)   (c)   (d)   (e)

12. Surgeon is to scalpel as painter is to
    (a) model (b) brush (c) flower (d) medicine

13. Which word completes the following series of words?
   president   nation   governor   state   mayor
   (a) United States   (b) city   (c) congress   (d) corporation

14. Circle is to semicircle as diameter is to
   (a) hypotenuse   (b) radius   (c) square   (d) triangle

15. Which of the following words does not belong in the series?
   (a) speech   (b) play   (c) talk   (d) hold   (e) run

16. If you have $100 in the bank for two years and the bank pays 6 percent interest per year (computed once annually), how much will you have at the end of two years?
   (a) $136.00   (b) $106.36   (c) $112.36   (d) $116.36   (e) none of these

17. Picture is to mural as song is to
   (a) melody   (b) opera   (c) piano   (d) painter

18. Fourteen men are on the bank of a river that they want to cross. They have a rowboat that requires two men for rowing and seats four additional persons. How many one-way crossings must the boat make to get all fourteen men across?
   (a) six   (b) four   (c) five   (d) three

19. The words in the box below are arranged in a logical order. Select the word that belongs where the question mark appears.

   | composer | listener | ? |
   | author | reader | story |

   (a) orchestra   (b) painter   (c) song   (d) novel

20. Butterfly is to caterpillar as frog is to
   (a) fish   (b) bird   (c) tadpole   (d) toad

21. If John is taller than Roger and Bill, and Roger is taller than Tom, and Tom is taller than Bill, then which of the following is also true?
   (a) Tom is taller than John   (b) Bill is taller than Roger   (c) Roger is smaller than Bill   (d) Roger is taller than Bill

22. Which of the following words does not belong in the series?
   (a) beautiful   (b) calm   (c) quickly   (d) proud   (e) interesting

23. A century is to 100 as a decade is to
   (a) 1000   (b) 10   (c) 20   (d) years

24. Surfeit means
   (a) loss   (b) survival   (c) excess   (d) fear

25. Which of the following does not belong in the series?

   (a)   (b)   (c)   (d)   (e)

26. Which of the following does not belong in the series?

   (a)   (b)   (c)   (d)   (e)

27. Which of the following does not belong in the series?

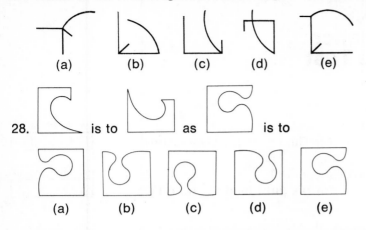

(a)   (b)   (c)   (d)   (e)

28.

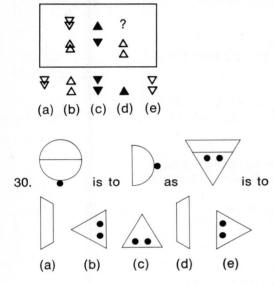

(a)   (b)   (c)   (d)   (e)

29. Select the drawing that belongs where the question mark appears.

(a) (b) (c) (d) (e)

30.

(a)   (b)   (c)   (d)   (e)

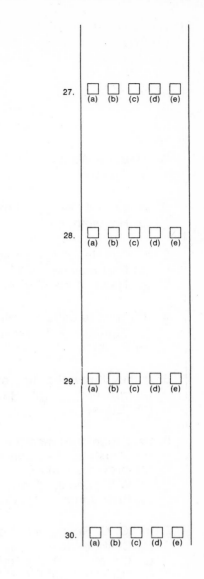

27. ☐ ☐ ☐ ☐ ☐
(a) (b) (c) (d) (e)

28. ☐ ☐ ☐ ☐ ☐
(a) (b) (c) (d) (e)

29. ☐ ☐ ☐ ☐ ☐
(a) (b) (c) (d) (e)

30. ☐ ☐ ☐ ☐ ☐
(a) (b) (c) (d) (e)

The Dove Counterbalance Intelligence Test

by Adrian Dove

1. "T-Bone Walker" got famous for playing what?
   (a) Trombone   (b) Piano   (c) "T-Flute"   (d) Guitar   (e) "Hambone"

   (a) (b) (c) (d) (e)
   1. ○ ○ ○ ○ ○

2. Whom did "Stagger Lee" kill (in the famous blues legend)?
   (a) His mother   (b) Frankie   (c) Johnny   (d) His girl friend   (e) Billy

   (a) (b) (c) (d) (e)
   2. ○ ○ ○ ○ ○

3. A "Gas Head" is a person who has a
   (a) Fast moving car   (b) Stable of "lace"   (c) Process
   (d) Habit of stealing cars   (e) Long jail record for arson

   (a) (b) (c) (d) (e)
   3. ○ ○ ○ ○ ○

4. If a man is called a "Blood," then he is a
   (a) Fighter   (b) Mexican-American   (c) Negro   (d) Hungry Hemophile
   (e) Redman or Indian

   (a) (b) (c) (d) (e)
   4. ○ ○ ○ ○ ○

5. If they throw the dice and "7" is showing on the top, what is facing down?
   (a) "Seven"   (b) "Snake eyes"   (c) "Boxcars"   (d) "Little Joes"
   (e) "Eleven"

   (a) (b) (c) (d) (e)
   5. ○ ○ ○ ○ ○

6. Jazz pianist Ahmad Jamal took an Arabic name after becoming really famous. Previously he had some fame with what he called his "slave name." What was his previous name?
   (a) Willie Lee Jackson   (b) LeRoi Jones   (c) Wilbur McDougal
   (d) Fritz Jones   (e) Andy Johnson

   (a) (b) (c) (d) (e)
   6. ○ ○ ○ ○ ○

7. In "C. C. Rider," what does "C. C." stand for?
   (a) Civil Service   (b) Church Council
   (c) County Circuit, preacher of an old-time rambler   (d) Country Club
   (e) "Cheating Charley" (the "Boxcar Gunsel")

   (a) (b) (c) (d) (e)
   7. ○ ○ ○ ○ ○

8. Cheap "chitlings" (not the kind you purchase at the frozen-food counter) will taste rubbery unless they are cooked long enough. How soon can you quit cooking them to eat and enjoy them?
   (a) 15 minutes   (b) 2 hours   (c) 24 hours
   (d) 1 week (on a low flame)   (e) 1 hour

   (a) (b) (c) (d) (e)
   8. ○ ○ ○ ○ ○

9. "Down Home" (the South) today, for the average "Soul Brother" who is picking cotton (in season from sunup until sundown), what is the average earning (take home) for one full day?
   (a) $0.75   (b) $1.65   (c) $3.50   (d) $5.00   (e) $12.00

   (a) (b) (c) (d) (e)
   9. ○ ○ ○ ○ ○

10. If a judge finds you guilty of "holding weed" (in California), what's the most he can give you?
    (a) Indeterminate (life)   (b) A nickel   (c) A dime   (d) A year in county
    (e) $100.00.

    (a) (b) (c) (d) (e)
    10. ○ ○ ○ ○ ○

11. "Bird" or "Yardbird" was the "jacket" that jazz lovers from coast to coast hung on
    (a) Lester Young   (b) Peggy Lee   (c) Benny Goodman
    (d) Charlie Parker   (e) "Birdman of Alcatraz"

    (a) (b) (c) (d) (e)
    11. ○ ○ ○ ○ ○

12. A "Hype" is a person who
    (a) Always says he feels sickly   (b) Has water on the brain   (c) Uses heroin
    (d) Is always riping and running   (e) Is always sick

    (a) (b) (c) (d) (e)
    12. ○ ○ ○ ○ ○

13. Mattle Mae Johnson is on the county. She has four children and her husband is now in jail for nonsupport, as he was unemployed and was not able to give her any money. Her welfare check is now $286.00 per month. Last night she went out with the biggest player in town. If she got pregnant, then nine months from now how much more will her welfare check be?
(a) $80.00   (b) $50.00   (c) $35.00   (d) $150.00   (e) $100.00

(a) (b) (c) (d) (e)
13. ○ ○ ○ ○ ○

14. "Hully Gully" came from
(a) "East Oakland"   (b) Fillmore   (c) Watts   (d) Harlem
(e) Motor City

(a) (b) (c) (d) (e)
14. ○ ○ ○ ○ ○

15. Where is Eldridge Cleaver?
(a) Harlem   (b) Algiers   (c) Cuba   (d) Dead

(a) (b) (c) (d)
15. ○ ○ ○ ○

16. The opposite of square is
(a) Round   (b) Up   (c) Down   (d) Hip   (e) Lame

(a) (b) (c) (d) (e)
16. ○ ○ ○ ○ ○

17. Do "The Beatles" have soul?
(a) Yes   (b) No   (c) Gee Whiz, or maybe

(a) (b) (c)
17. ○ ○ ○

18. A "Handkerchief Head" is
(a) A cool cat   (b) A porter   (c) An "Uncle Tom"   (d) A hoddi
(e) A "preacher"

(a) (b) (c) (d) (e)
18. ○ ○ ○ ○ ○

19. What are the "Dixie Hummingbirds"?
(a) A part of the KKK   (b) A swamp disease   (c) A modern Gospel group
(d) A Mississippi Negro, para-military strike force

(a) (b) (c) (d)
19. ○ ○ ○ ○

20. "Jet" is
(a) An "East Oakland" motorcycle club
(b) One of the gangs in West Side Story   (c) A news and gossip magazine
(d) A way of life for the very rich

(a) (b) (c) (d)
20. ○ ○ ○ ○

For 21–24, fill in the missing word or words that sound best.

21. "Tell it like it
(a) Thinks I am"   (b) Baby"   (c) Try"   (d) Is"   (e) Y'all"

(a) (b) (c) (d) (e)
21. ○ ○ ○ ○ ○

22. "You've got to get up early in the morning if you want to
(a) Catch the worms"   (b) Be healthy, wealthy, and wise"
(c) Try to fool me"   (d) Fare well"   (e) Be the first one on the street"

(a) (b) (c) (d) (e)
22. ○ ○ ○ ○ ○

23. "Walk together, children,
(a) Don't you get weary—there's a great camp meeting"
(b) For we shall overcome"
(c) For the family that walks together talks together"
(d) By your patience you will win your souls" (Luke 21:19)
(e) Find the things that are above, not the things that are on Earth" (Col. 3:3)

(a) (b) (c) (d) (e)
23. ○ ○ ○ ○ ○

24. "Money don't get everything, it's true
(a) But I don't have none and I'm so blue"
(b) But what it don't get I can't use"   (c) So make with what you've got"
(d) But I don't know that and neither do you"

(a) (b) (c) (d)
24. ○ ○ ○ ○

25. "Bo-Didley" is a
(a) Camp for children   (b) Cheap wine   (c) Singer   (d) New dance
(e) Mojo call

(a) (b) (c) (d) (e)
25. ○ ○ ○ ○ ○

26. Which word is most out of place here?
    (a) Splib   (b) Blood   (c) Gray   (d) Spook   (e) Black

27. How much does a "short-dog" cost?
    (a) $0.15   (b) $2.00   (c) $0.35   (d) $0.05   (e) $0.86 + tax

28. True or False: A "Pimp" is also a young man who lies around all day.
    (a) True   (b) False

29. If a Pimp is up tight with a woman who gets California State aid, what does he mean when he talks about "Mother's Day"?
    (a) Second Sunday in May   (b) Third Sunday in June
    (c) First of every month   (d) None of these
    (e) First and fifteenth of every month

30. Many people say that "Juneteenth" (June 19) should be made legal holiday because this was the day when
    (a) The slaves were freed in Jamaica   (b) The slaves were freed in California
    (c) Martin Luther King was born   (d) Booker T. Washington died
    (e) The slaves were freed in Texas

Credits and Acknowledgments

2—John Oldenkamp/IBOL; 8—Steve Mc-Carroll/IBOL; 13—Tom Lewis; 18—William MacDonald/IBOL; 21 and 22—Tom Lewis; 27 and 29—Pamela Morehouse; 38—Steve McCarroll/IBOL; 41—From J. Hochberg and E. McAlister, "Quantitative Approach to Figural Goodness," *Journal of Experimental Psychology,* Vol. 46, 1953, pp. 361-364; 46—Harry Crosby/Photophile; 49 and 51—Tom Lewis; 57—Stan Solledar; 59—(top) Tom Lewis, (bottom) Stan Solledar: 60—William Noonan; 68—Paul Slick; 69—(bottom) John Dawson, after S. Polyak, *The Retina,* University of Chicago Press, 1941; 71, 73, 76-77—John Dawson; 79—William MacDonald/IBOL; 82—Rowland Scherman; 85—John Oldenkamp/IBOL; 86—Robert Van Doren; 91-97—Karl Nicholason; 106—(a) and (c) Al Boliska, *The World's Worst Jokes,* Mc-Clelland & Stewart, Ltd.; 107—(a) © by Bill Adler, all rights reserved, (b) Art Linkletter, *I Wish I'd Said That,* Doubleday; 124—Nancy Chase; 126, 131—John Dawson; 133—Courtesy of Ketchum, MacLeod and Grove, Inc.; 142—Robert Van Doren; 151-153—From I. Bell, *Involvement in Society Today,* CRM Books, 1971; 155-157—Adrian Dove.